TALL SHIPS
HANDBOOK

AMANDA BUTCHER

AMBERLEY

'And all I ask is a tall ship and a star to steer her by.'
John Masefield

My thanks to MAX, Simon Stenning and www.tallshipstock.com for the photos they have
each provided.

First published 2014

Amberley Publishing
The Hill, Stroud
Gloucestershire, GL5 4EP

www.amberley-books.com

British Library Cataloguing in Publication Data.
A catalogue record for this book is available from the British Library.

ISBN 978 1 4456 1889 0
E-book ISBN 978 1 4456 1868 5

Typeset in 10pt on 12pt Minion Pro.
Typesetting and Origination by Amberley Publishing.
Printed in the UK.

CONTENTS

WHY YOU NEED THIS BOOK

There are several reasons why you might need this book. Perhaps you are a visitor to a Maritime Festival or one of the Tall Ships Race ports and want to know a bit more.

Maybe you have always dreamed of sailing on a tall ship and would like to find out which ships offer berths to people with little or no experience.

You may be someone who travels the world and gets a chance to see these beautiful vessels at sea or in port and realise you want to learn more about them.

Whatever the reason for reading this book I hope that you will find something of interest. Some of the ships have provided the background text and pictures themselves; for those that haven't I apologise if my research has not found the latest information. Please feel free to send me anything I have missed ready for the next edition (tallshipbook@aol.com).

The reason that I have put this reference guide together is because since I was first involved in tall ships I have been looking for a book like this and have discovered that it does not exist. There are plenty of glossy coffee table books with beautiful pictures and even whole books dedicated to a single ship but nothing to use as a field guide for those with no technical knowledge.

Crew relaxing on *Eye of the Wind*.

At sea on *Stad Amsterdam*.

Cabin on *Oosterschelde*.

WHAT IS A TALL SHIP?

A tall ship is not a specifically defined type of sailing vessel. Most of us use the term to mean a large traditionally rigged sailing vessel, whether or not it is technically a 'ship'.

For many people, the term tall ship makes them think about historical vessels, perhaps museum pieces such as *Cutty Sark* in London or *Dar Pormoza* in Gdansk. Many maritime museums around the world have some wonderful vessels on display; a few, such as the *James Craig* in Sydney, are still seagoing vessels.

Surprisingly though, there are still many square-rigged sailing vessels sailing the oceans of the world, and many of them are not that old. Today's definitions of the tall ships come from the need to provide a fair system of handicapping for the Tall Ships Races by the organisers, Sail Training International.

The introduction of the Tall Ships Races in 1956 (see frontispiece picture), and the associated maritime festivals that have grown up since, have helped keep these vessels alive. Many of the vessels that enter these races offer a form of adventurous training for young people, called 'sail training', so they earn their living by selling berths on board. Some vessels will take adults, including those with disabilities. However, other factors include the requirement for navies from around the world to teach traditional seafaring skills to their young cadets.

The square riggers and the largest ships (those over 40 m in length) all fall into Class A. Class B vessels are those with a traditional rig but under 40 m. This book concentrates on the Class A tall ships; even so they are not all included. In particular, those based in the USA and Canada that do not travel in international waters are not here; they could fill another book on their own.

Within Class A there is a variety of ship designs, and later chapters will help you discover more about them. You will find information about the different types in the section called 'How to Use This Book'.

Some of the ships are replicas, new ships that have been built to look like an historical vessel, either for use in a film or to preserve maritime history. There are also a number of older vessels that have been restored but, most importantly, there is also an increasing number of brand-new Class A tall ships being built. Instead of being a dying breed, there are more every year.

The *James Craig* under sail.

Cutty Sark landlocked.

The modern Tall Ships Races.

SEEING THE TALL SHIPS

A tall ship under sail at sea is a wonderful sight. Having the chance to see large gatherings of them is something that attracts tens of thousands of people.

In 1956 a small group of people got together to organise what was intended to be a 'glorious farewell to the age of sail'. They organised a race from Torbay to Lisbon which they expected to be the last time a significant number of tall ships would ever be seen together. The history of the race is now well documented but briefly the event turned out to be so popular that another was arranged and another…

In 2006, the Fiftieth Anniversary race was staged over the same route and attracted over 100 vessels.

These days the races are not only annual events, they take place all over the world. In 2013 there were races arranged in the Baltic, the Mediterranean and from Australia to New Zealand. Between 2014 and 2018 there are races planned to visit Scandinavia, the UK, Canada, the USA, Bermuda, Southern Europe and the Black Sea ports.

The races are organised by Sail Training International with the support of national agencies and participating ports. As well as ensuring that the events are run safely, it also means that the race dates around the world are coordinated to ensure that the ships can take part in as many of them as possible. It also ensures that no two ports organise their events for the same weekend.

The ports which host the races bid many years in advance for the opportunity, as the associated festivals bring in large numbers of visitors and offer a boost to the local economy. The festivals usually include shoreside entertainment such as crew parades, concerts and fireworks. For the visiting public there is the chance to visit the ships when they have 'open ship' days, giving everyone the chance to get a taste of life on board.

With a big entertainment programme and often the opportunity to see the ships leave in their 'parade of sail', most visitors stay for a couple of days.

For the ship operators there will also be the opportunity to offer places on the next leg of their journey to young people from the local area. The benefits of sail training are enormous and whether you're a youngster looking for adventure or someone who would benefit from personal development, there will be a ship offering the right sort of programme. It's not just limited to young people though; several of the ships take adult crew members, including those with disabilities. Some offer seafaring training but most ask for nothing but a sense of adventure and a willingness to join in with the day-to-day tasks involved with working and living aboard a sailing ship.

Almost every participating country now has their own Sail Training organisation, working with the ships that visit as well as those that have their home ports in that country. To find out more about events in your own area, or for information about how to sail on the tall ships, it's a good place to start. All of the contact details can be found from links on the Sail Training International website under the 'Get on board' link.

Learning the ropes.

Working aloft.

Port days.

Crew Parades are not all the same!

Crew Parade.

Concerts.

Alexander von Humboldt 2 under full sail.

HOW TO USE THIS BOOK

The aim of the book is first to help you identify any Class A tall ship that you come across and then to tell you a little more about it. Of course the easiest way is to look for the name and then use the index. Often, however, it can be difficult to see the name; it could be on the bow, along the side or even on the stern (the rear) of the ship – only visible from behind. It may not even be written in English!

The first thing to do is to try to identify the design. Technically these vessels are only ships if they have three masts or more and are square rigged on all masts. (That means that they have yards carrying square sails on all the masts.)

It can be very confusing the first time you realise that most of the 'tall ships' aren't ships at all! You can always get away with calling them vessels but that doesn't sound quite as interesting.

A quick look at some of the diagrams here will give you a pretty good idea of the type of any 'ship' you are looking at without even seeing its name – you'll soon know your Brigs from your Barques! Once you have worked out what type you have found just flick through the section in the Ship Directory to check out the size and type of sails and you should be able to narrow it down. With a bit of extra information, like the colour of the hull or even the port of registration, you'll soon feel like an expert.

You will see that there are other sails as well as those that are square rigged and they all have general names; the ones like normal yacht sails are the 'fore and aft' sails and others, carried on a boom-like device, are 'gaff rigged'.

The data table for each ship contains the following information:

Crew	Cadets/Trainees	POR	Type	LOA
This is the number of permanent or professional crew	These are the people who join for an individual voyage. For some vessels there is a higher number allowed on a (non-residential) daysail	Port of Registration: The Port where the ship is officially registered, not always the home port	New build or replica or restoration	The length (length over all) including the bowsprit

This diagram shows the tall ship *Pelican*, an unusual example of a Barquentine (three-masted with one mast square rigged).

However, it shows a good variety of sails. The three masts are known as the foremast (nearest the bow), the main mast (in this case the middle one) and the mizzen mast (nearest the stern). For a complete list of sails and other rigging parts, see the back of the book.

Key: (note that some sails have names that reflect the mast they are associated with)

1. Outer jib; 2. Jib; 3. Fore staysail; 4. Main staysail; 5. Gaff staysail; 6. Royal; 7. T'gallant; 8. Topsail; 9. Course; 10. Mizzen topsail; 11. Spanker.

Except for sister ships (those that have been built to the same design), you will find that the ships all have slightly different sail plans. For example, even if two ships are both Brigs they may have a different number of yards carrying the square sails or a different configuration of fore and aft sails.

By studying the sail plan and comparing it to the pictures in the ship directory, you will be able to quickly narrow down the possibilities when trying to identify a vessel.

A good way to start is to look at the number of masts. None of the Class A ships just have a single mast, so we start with two-masted vessels.

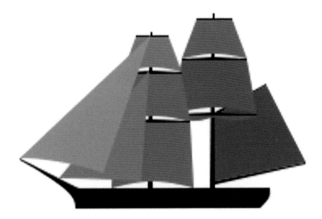

A Brig has two masts and is square rigged on both.

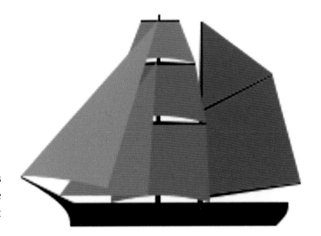

A Brigantine also has two masts but is square rigged on only the foremast (the name for the mast nearest the front or bow).

However, there is a large number of ships that have two masts but are Class B vessels, and the next section of the Ship Directory has more information about them. Some ships that would be considered Class B because of their rig are over 40 m and so are classified as Class A vessels.

If a ship has three masts it will probably be a Barque, a Barquentine or a fully rigged ship.

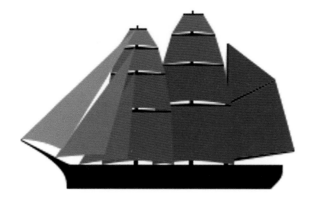

A Barque is square rigged on all but its aft mast (the one nearest the stern).

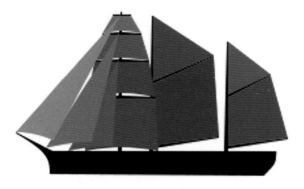

A Barquentine is square rigged on only one mast (usually the foremast)

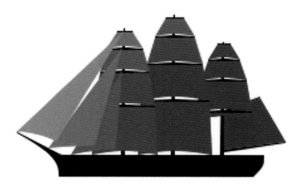

Three-masted fully rigged ship.

Ships with four or more masts are likely to be four-masted Barques or fully rigged ships but there are a few special cases; check the section of the Ship Directory for more information.

Sedov, a 4-masted barque.

As well as sail plans, other things to look for are nationality, which you may be able to work out from any flags flown at the stern or from the port of registration, which will usually be displayed on the stern, and, if you have two ships together, the relative size may give a clue.

For each ship I have offered a 'Tip' to help with your identification. There is also a 'bluff your way' fact – a piece of obscure or unusual information about the ship.

Ship Directory:
Two-Masted Vessels

Most of the Class A tall ships with two masts will be either Brigs or Brigantines.

However, there is a huge number of two-masted Class B vessels and it is easy to be caught out. Although there are many designs for Class B vessels, the two-masted ones can generally be put into one of two categories – a Ketch or a Schooner. The simple way to tell the difference is the relative height of the two masts.

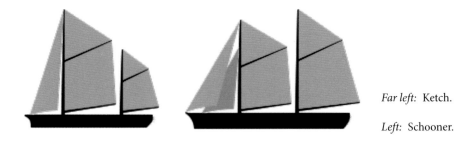

Far left: Ketch.

Left: Schooner.

Just to add to the complication, some Class B vessels may have up to three square sails at the top of their foremast. An example is the Class B Topsail Schooner *Brabander* from Lithuania. However, if any vessel is over 40 m in length, regardless of its sail plan, it becomes a Class A ship purely by virtue of its size!

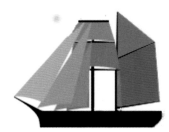

Topsail Schooner.

Brabander.

Enterprize

Australian-registered Topsail Schooner

Website: www.enterprize.org.au

Crew	Cadets/Trainees	POR	Type	LOA
6	9	Melbourne	Replica	27m

Launched in 1997 the ship is a replica of John Pascoe Fawkner's Schooner *Enterprize* – the ship that sailed from Van Diemen's Land (Tasmania) in 1835 with the first permanent white settlers who founded what is now the city of Melbourne.

The original vessel was built in Hobart in 1830. At that time most bulk cargo was transported by sea, and she carried cargo such as coal and, on one occasion, over 180 sheep.

The replica ship has two functions: a Living History programme telling the story of Melbourne's beginning and a programme which offers people a taste of life aboard an eighteenth-century trading ship through a sail-training and coastal voyage programme open to everyone. Working with local schools, young people spend time in the history classroom and then have a short sail-training experience sailing on board *Enterprize*.

'Bluff your way' fact: It was decided that the replica would use the same materials that were used in the original ship where possible.

This meant the sails could not be machine sewn from modern synthetic sailcloth but were hand sewn from flax cloth imported from Scotland.

Tip: her name and port of registration are shown on her stern.

Re-enactors in 1830s costumes for Melbourne Day.

Enterprize off her home port of Melbourne.

An unusual picture of *Enterprize* with the *Bark Europa* during the Dutch ship's visit to Australia in 2013.

Eye of the Wind

UK-registered, German-operated Brig

Website: www.eyeofthewind.net

Crew	Cadets/Trainees	POR	Type	LOA
10	16	Jersey	Restoration	40.2m

Originally built as the Topsail Schooner *Friedrich* in 1911, *Eye of the Wind* has had a varied history. Her name was changed several times over the years, and she has been called *Sam*, *Merry* and *Rose-Marie* at various times. She also sailed as a Brigantine in the 1970s before her latest refit. She is now owned and operated by a German media group and offers sail-training voyages, leadership training and private charters.

During her career she has sailed in most parts of the world but these days she does most of her sailing in German coastal waters but occasionally joins the tall ship fleet for races and festivals.

Tip: *Eye of the Wind* is unusual for a Class A vessel in that she carries tan-coloured sails which were fitted for one of her film roles and then retained. Even when not under sail you can usually see the colour of the sails, which will help to identify her.

'Bluff your way' fact: The ship's bell bears the words 'Where we go one we go all', which is a quote from the film *White Squall* in which *Eye of the Wind* played the part of the ill-fated ship *Albatross*.

Above: Eye of the Wind under sail in light winds.

Top right: Figurehead.

Above right: Crew working on the bowsprit of *Eye of the Wind* clearly showing the tan sails.

Right: Eye of the Wind ship's bell.

Fryderyk Chopin

Polish Brig

Crew	Cadets/Trainees	POR	Type	LOA
8	45	Szczecin	New build	55.5m

With a length of 55.5 m (including the bowsprit) *Fryderyk Chopin*, named after the nineteenth-century composer, is probably the largest Brig currently sailing. She was completed in 1992 and is one of a number of tall ships built in Gdansk shipyards. She is operated by the European School of Law and Administration in Warsaw and has been used to support various sail-training programmes including Schools Afloat (Canada) and the Baltic University Programme.

Her topside is white with a red waterline, mirroring the colours of the Polish flag. She has no figurehead.

She operates worldwide with voyages in the Caribbean and Europe; some voyages are open for individuals to book berths. She is a regular participant in the European Tall Ships Races.

Tip: She has 6 yards (and hence six square sails) on each of her masts, a particularly unusual configuration.

'Bluff your way' fact: She hit the news in 2010 when she was dismasted close to the Scilly Isles on her way to the Caribbean. Fortunately she was still close enough to the mainland to be towed back to Falmouth, UK. The captain was unable to use the engines for fear of fouling the rigging in the propellers.

Fryderyk Chopin dismasted in 2010 (photo courtesy RNLI).

Under sail.

Kapitan Glowacki

Polish Brigantine

Website: www.coz.com.pl

Crew	Cadets/Trainees	POR	Type	LOA
6	16	Szczecin	Restoration	29.7m

The vessel was abandoned after the war and found lying in the sand by some Polish people in the north-west corner of Poland. She was quickly renovated and in 1946 became a gaff-rigged ketch serving as a training vessel for maritime schools in Poland during the 1950s, 1960s and part of the 1970s. During this time she bore the name *Henry Rotkowski*.

In the 1980s she was rebuilt again, this time as a Brigantine, and became a school ship for the Polish Sailing Association. She was given her present name in 1997 in memory of Captain Vladimir Glowacki (1910–1955), who was a great supporter of sailing in Poland. She is now the flagship of the Polish Sailing Association. She sails mostly in the Baltic and North Sea participating in Tall Ships Races and festivals in her home areas.

Tip: At a little under 30 m she is one of the smallest European Class A vessels and distinguishable by her suite of tan sails and brightly coloured ropes.

'Bluff your way' fact: The history of *Kapitan Glowacki* before the war is still not known exactly. It was originally thought that she had been a fishing boat, but more recent evidence suggests that she was built as a military surveillance cutter and was possibly named *Fordel* at one time.

Kapitan Glowacki's pins and ropes.

Lady Nelson

Australian Brig

Website: www.ladynelson.org.au

Crew	Cadets/Trainees	POR	Type	LOA
6	10	Hobart	Replica	16.7m

Launched in 1988, *Lady Nelson* is a full-size replica of the original 1799 Deptford-built (London, UK) Brig, HMS *Lady Nelson*. She generally carries out day sails on the River Derwent from her home port of Hobart, offering an introductory tall ship experience, with passengers able to help set sails, take a turn at the helm or just enjoy the feel of a traditional sailing ship. For the more adventurous there are weekend and longer trips, which aim to provide a full sail-training experience.

For special occasions and significant anniversaries she ventures across the Bass Strait to the Australian mainland. In 2013 she sailed to Sydney as part of the tall ship festivals celebrating the Royal Australian Navy's centenary, and took part in the International Fleet Review.

Tip: At a little under 17 m she is one of the smallest Class A ships in the world and she has a distinctive white and mustard hull.

'Bluff your way' fact: When the international tall ships visited Hobart in 2013, UK tall ship *Lord Nelson* and *Lady Nelson* met for the first time.

Lady Nelson alongside in her home port of Hobart; in the background a glimpse of *Windeward Bound*'s masts can be seen.

Lady Nelson under sail (photo courtesy of the Tasmanian Sail Training Association).

Mercedes

Dutch Brig

Website: www.sailingship-mercedes.com

Crew	Cadets/Trainees	POR	Type	LOA
Varied	36 (cruise) 140 (daysail)	Amsterdam	Restoration	50m

Originally built, in steel, as a fishing trawler in 1958, *Mercedes*'s major restoration was completed in 2005. She was rigged as a Brig and was primarily designed for day cruises, evening cruises and receptions moored in a port rather than for sail training. When she was given the name *Mercedes* in 2005 it was the seventh name the vessel had held.

During the summer she attends most of the European festivals, from the Mediterranean to the Baltic, and her schedule allows her to earn her keep offering charters for entertaining. She also offers cruises with some limited opportunities for sail training when taking part in the Tall Ship Races.

Tip: Her name is on a white plate on the bow of her black hull, and in black lettering on her white stern; her bowsprit is also white.

'Bluff your way' fact: In 2013 she was put up for sale for €3.9M.

Decked out for corporate
entertainment.

Morgenster

Dutch Brig

Website: www.zeilBrig.org

Crew	Cadets/Trainees	POR	Type	LOA
10	36	Den Helder	Restoration	48m

Morgenster, meaning Morning Star, was originally the fishing vessel *Vrouwe Maria*, built in 1918; after several new leases of life she was restored in 2008 as a sail-training vessel. She is privately owned by Marion and Harry Muter and is regularly entered in European Tall Ship Races and festivals. The rigging is based on the American clippers used during the War of Independence.

She focuses on sail training during her summer voyages and, as well as offering opportunities to individuals to sail, she is used by the Royal Netherlands Navy for training. In the winter she stays on her berth in Den Helder, close to the Naval Museum. Her figurehead is a seahorse with a woman riding on its back.

Tip: Her name is in red lettering on a gold ribbon design on the stern (reflecting the gold line along her hull) and black on white on the bow.

'Bluff your way' fact: In the early 1980s *Morgenster* was fitted out to be the vessel for the ill-fated pirate radio station Radio Del Mare, which never really enjoyed any success.

At sea.

Her name on the stern.

And the bow.

Rah Naward

Pakistani Brig

Website: www.paknavy.gov.pk

Crew	Cadets/Trainees	POR	Type	LOA
12	48	Karachi	New build	59.35m

Rah Naward (meaning swift mover) was commissioned into the Pakistan Navy in 2010. She was previously the UK sail-training vessel *Prince William*, owned and operated by the UK charity The Tall Ships Youth Trust, and a regular at races and festivals. Her sister ship *Stavros Niarchos* remained in the UK.

Rah Naward is the first sail-training vessel owned by the Pakistan Navy and she represents a growing trend for large navies to use traditional sailing vessels as part of their seafarers' training. She is expected to take part in international Tall Ships Races and festivals as part of her programme.

Tip: She has retained the traditional black-and-white paint scheme representing the old gun ports from her days as *Prince William*.

'Bluff your way' fact: Although the first time the hull was launched was as *Prince William*, she previously had been given the name *Neptun Baroness* and was destined to be a luxury sailing cruise ship for the Caribbean.

Rah Naward alongside in Hull flying the flag of Pakistan.

Under sail as *Prince William*.

Rah Naward under sail. (Photo courtesy Tallshipstock.com)

Roald Amundsen

German Brig

Website: www.sailtraining.de

Crew	Cadets/Trainees	POR	Type	LOA
17	32	Eckernforde	Restoration	50.2m

Roald Amundsen was built in 1952 as the steel-hulled ship *Vilm*, originally intended as a fishing vessel. However, before she was completed, the plans changed and she operated first as a tanker and then as a bilge-water carrier. In 1992 the hull was bought for a German society called 'Learn to live on sailing ships' (Lebenlernen auf Segelschiffen). She was rigged as a Brig for use as a sail-training vessel and named for the Norwegian polar explorer, but is often just referred to as Roald.

She is operated on a not-for profit basis and is supported by a large number of volunteers. Berths are available year round as she spends the summer months in Europe, often including the Tall Ships Races, and then sails to the Canaries or Caribbean for the winter season.

Tip: She has no figurehead and carries her German sailing vessel registration number TS G508 on one of the sails on her foremast.

'Bluff your way' fact: Everyone on board pays a contribution towards their berth, even the professional crew who are all unpaid volunteers.

Roald Amundsen under sail.

Roald Amundsen during a visit to the USA and Canada in 2010 when she sailed in the Great Lakes (seen flying the Canadian "courtesy" flag).

Royalist

UK Brig

Website: www.squareriggerclub.org.uk (a supporters' club, not the official Marine Society and Sea Cadets site)

Crew	Cadets/Trainees	POR	Type	LOA
8	24	Portsmouth	New build	29.52m

The TS *Royalist* was launched in 1971 and is the sail-training ship for the UK youth organisation, the Sea Cadets. It is likely that 2014 will be her last year of operation, as a replacement training ship has been commissioned and is being built in Spain. *Royalist* may well then be sold and appear with a new name somewhere in the world. The new ship is expected to be called *Royalist II*.

She sails year round and mostly takes groups for a week at a time; as a result her operating area is generally limited to the south coast of the UK, the Channel Islands and Northern France. However, during the European Tall Ships Races she undertakes longer trips and visits more countries to match the race and festival schedule.

As a figurehead, she has a Sea Cadet Badge held by two cadets, one male and one female.

Tip: As she often sails with Masters who are members of the Royal Navy Reserve, she frequently is seen flying a blue ensign rather than the UK red ensign.

'Bluff your way' fact: *Royalist* was designed by Colin Mudie from the UK, who also designed the Jubilee Sailing Trust's *Lord Nelson*, the Indian ship *Tarangini* and the Australian *Young Endeavour*, among others.

Above: *Royalist* under sail.

Right: *Royalist* bow.

Søren Larsen

Cook Islands Brigantine

Website: www.sorenlarsen.com

Crew	Cadets/Trainees	POR	Type	LOA
13	22	Avatiu	Restoration	44.2m

Built from oak in Denmark at the Søren Larsen & Sons shipyard, she was a working cargo ship until 1972. In 1978 she was rescued and restored by a British family, and used mainly for film work. Between 1982 and 1985 she was chartered to the UK charity The Jubilee Sailing Trust and used to develop a tall ship sailing programme that would be suitable for both able-bodied people and those with physical disabilities.

In 1987/88 she joined a number of European tall ships that sailed to Australia as part of the re-enactment and celebrations for the bicentennial of the arrival of the First Fleet.

Although she returned to Europe as part of two circumnavigations of the globe, she was then based out of New Zealand, although registered in UK, until relocating to her current home port of Sydney in 2011.

Still privately owned, she offers a combination of day sails out of Sydney and longer voyages to the Pacific Islands to people aged sixteen to eighty-five.

Tip: Her name plate is a wooden board along her white bow.

'Bluff your way' fact: Her restoration was largely paid for from fees for film appearances, which include *The French Lieutenant's Woman* and *Shackleton*, and the British TV series *The Onedin Line*.

Søren Larsen under sail.

Alongside in Sydney.

Stavros Niarchos

UK Brig

Website: www.tallships.org

Crew	Cadets/Trainees	POR	Type	LOA
6	62	London	New build	59.4m

Stavros Niarchos is one of two sister ships that until recently were both operated by The Tall Ships Youth Trust. Her sister ship, *Prince Willliam*, was sold to the Pakistan Navy in 2010 and is now sailing with the name *Rah Naward*. *Stavros Niarchos* is also up for sale but still operating and taking part in races and festivals. Like *Prince William*, the almost completed hull was bought from Germany, where it was originally called *Neptun Princess*. She was rigged as a Brig and launched in 2000. Voyages are categorised by age groups, starting with twelve to fifteen year olds and progressing all the way to adult voyages.

The Tall Ships Youth Trust concentrates on offering opportunities to disadvantaged young people, through their sail-training programmes on *Stavros Niarchos* and their smaller Challenger yachts. Although registered in London, Portsmouth is considered her home port.

Tip: Her paint scheme has the same imitation gun ports as her sister ship – look out for the UK ensign.

'Bluff your way' fact: The Tall Ships Youth Trust was founded in the 1950s and was responsible for the organisation of the first Tall Ships Races.

Under sail with *Prince William* in the background.

Stavros Niarchos dressed overall off Aarhus with the tall ships race fleet (*Alexander von Humboldt II* and *Shtandart* in the background).

Tolkien

Dutch two-masted Topsail Schooner

Website: www.restchart.com

Crew	Cadets/Trainees	POR	Type	LOA
10	32	Amsterdam	Restoration	41.7m

She was originally launched in 1964 as the German tug *Dierkow*, and was converted to a sailing ship in 1994 after being bought by the van der Rest family, who still own her. As a Topsail Schooner with a length of 41.7 m, including her bowsprit, she is only just big enough to be in Class A. Although it is possible to sail overnight on her, most of her season is spent on day sails and private charter. As a result she does not enter the races but can usually be found at festivals and maritime events in the North Sea area.

Tip: Her white hull has black trim and her name can be found on her bow, with the 'J R' in a smaller font than 'Tolkien'.

'Bluff your way' fact: Although usually referred to as Tolkien, her full registered name is *J R Tolkien*, although she is named after the writer J. R. R. Tolkien.

The tug *Dierkow*.

J R Tolkien off Bremerhaven.

Tolkien's bow with her name.

Tre Kronor af Stockholm

Sweden Brig

Website: www.Briggentrekronor.se

Crew	Cadets/Trainees	POR	Type	LOA
8	12	Stockholm	Replica	45m

Tre Kronor is a replica of the Swedish Navy cargo ship, the Brig *Gladan*, which operated between 1857 and 1924. Built from wood using traditional shipbuilding methods, she was named in 2005 by her patron, Crown Princess Victoria of Sweden, although she did not undertake her maiden voyage until 2008. The ship's name means 'Three Crowns of Stockholm', representing the Swedish national symbol. The wooden name plate on her stern carries the name, written just as Tre Kronor over the port name Stockholm.

Her summer programme is a mixture of sail training, including Tall Ships Races, and day sails, and she is seen as a cultural ambassador for Stockholm. She returns to her home port for the winter.

Tip: Her unusual colouring and low profile make her easy to spot even from a distance.

'Bluff your way' fact: In order to raise money to start the construction, 200 shares at 4,000 Swedish Kronor each were sold. This was supplemented by a grant of 150,000 Kronor from the City of Stockholm. Nowadays the Tre Kronor Supporters group has over 4,000 members.

Tre Kronor af Stockholm with *Kapitan Borchart* (a Class B vessel).

Heading away.

Windeward Bound

Australian Brigantine

Website: www.windewardbound.com

Crew	Cadets/Trainees	POR	Type	LOA
7	9	Hobart	New build	33m

Windeward Bound is based on plans for an 1848 Boston-built Topsail Schooner, which was first seen in a long-out-of-print book on ship design. After extensive research, the full-size line drawings were unearthed at the Smithsonian Institute in Washington DC. The name of the new ship comes from the builder of the original ship, Edward Winde, rather than the expression 'windward'.

She was launched in 1996 and is operated by the specially set-up Windeward Bound Trust, with the aim of working with disadvantaged youths and young offenders from Tasmania, offering sail-training opportunities and educational programmes.

She has sailed around Australia and to New Zealand, although she has not yet visited the USA, which was a promised voyage in return for use of the plans. Like most of the Australian tall ships, she took part in the 2013 Royal Australian Navy centenary events.

Tip: She has a mustard-coloured band along the upper hull.

'Bluff your way' fact: The original concept for *Windeward Bound* was inspired by a sailing vessel called *New Endeavour*, seen by a young Australian Navy sailor in 1965. Sadly *New Endeavour* was broken up in 1987; however, she lives on, as her masts, yards, some of her sails, her anchors, anchor windlass and anchor cables were all used in the construction of *Windeward Bound*. That sailor now sails as Master of *Windeward Bound*.

At sea.

Windeward Bound in Cockle Bay, Sydney
for the Royal Australian Navy Centenary,
2013.

Wylde Swan

Dutch two-masted Topsail Schooner

Website: www.wyldeswan.com

Crew	Cadets/Trainees	POR	Type	LOA
12	36	Makkum	Restoration	62m

Built in Kiel, the hull of *Wylde Swan* started life as a steam ship, the 'herring hunter' *Jemo*, in the 1920s, working off the Shetland Islands bringing the fish from the fishing grounds to shore for market. The ship was decommissioned sometime in the late twentieth century and changed ownership several times before being taken on by Willem Slighting.

She was converted to a Topsail Schooner and relaunched in 2010 as a sail-training vessel. Since then she has participated in many European maritime festivals and events, as well as taking part in the Tall Ships Races. Her programme includes voyages in the North Sea and Baltic in the summer, and she spends the winters in the Caribbean.

Tip: Her name is shown in red on her black hull along the bow and on the stern.

'Bluff your way' fact: At 62 m she is the world's largest two-masted Topsail Schooner and longer than a number of the three-masted ships.

Wylde Swan at sea.

Wylde Swan alongside in Aarhus in 2013.

Young Endeavour

Australian Brigantine

Website: www.youngendeavour.gov.au

Crew	Cadets/Trainees	POR	Type	LOA
9	24	Sydney	New build	44m

Young Endeavour is operated by the Royal Australian Navy, although the administration is supported by a civilian team. The professional crew on board are all specially trained Australian Navy personnel, and the young people are selected from all over Australia after applying for places through a ballot scheme.

Each year one young person from New South Wales who has been on board is selected to take part in an international exchange with the UK, and travels to Europe to sail on a UK sail-training vessel, often with the Jubilee Sailing Trust.

Although *Young Endeavour* generally operates along the east and south coast of Australia, she has ventured further afield as well. In 1992 she circumnavigated the world as part of commemorations of the 500th anniversary of Columbus's discovery of the New World, and she has visited New Zealand on several occasions.

Tip: She has a short bowsprit, and as a Navy vessel flies the Australian white ensign.

'Bluff your way' fact: *Young Endeavour*, designed by Colin Mudie, was built in the UK as a gift from the UK to the government and people of Australia to celebrate the Australian bicentenary in 1988. On her delivery voyage she was sailed from UK to Australia with a crew of UK and Australian young people as part of the re-enactment of the arrival of the First Fleet into Sydney.

Under sail.

In Sydney Harbour with bare poles.

SHIP DIRECTORY: THREE-MASTED VESSELS

Most of the Class A tall ships with three masts will be Barques, Barquentines or fully rigged ships.

There are a few three-masted Class B vessels, but not many, because if they are big enough to have three masts they are likely to be over the 40-m length that would put them into Class A.

However, one example of a three-masted Class B Schooner is *Ingo* from Sweden; with a length of 37.8 m she just stays in Class B.

Ingo – Class B three-masted schooner.

Gulden Leeuw – Class A topsail schooner.

As with the two-masted vessels, there are also some ships with sail plans that would usually be Class B that make it into Class A because they are over 40 m – the three-masted Topsail Schooner *Gulden Leeuw* from the Netherlands is one example.

Alexander von Humboldt II

German three-masted Barque

Website: www.alex-2.de

Crew	Cadets/Trainees	POR	Type	LOA
25	54	Bremerhaven	New build	64.73m

Like her predecessor, the *Alexander Von Humboldt*, she is affectionately referred to as Alex or more properly Alex 2. She was built in Bremerhaven in 2011 and is operated by the Deutsche Stiftung Sail Training, which is a German non-profit organisation. Her main function is to promote traditional seamanship and teamwork, predominantly for young people aged fourteen and above, although places on board are also open to adults up to age seventy-five.

She is a regular entrant in the European Tall Ships Races and usually spends some time each year near her home port of Bremerhaven. Her recent winter voyages have included visits to Brazil, Mexico and the Caribbean.

Tip: Alex 2 is easy to identify because of her distinctive green hull. The original Alex also carried green sails, but sadly this has not been continued on Alex 2.

'Bluff your way' fact: The tradition of green comes from original sponsorship by Becks Beer.

Taken during the 2013 Tall Ship Race en route from Aarhus to Helsinki, this picture shows her struggling with her main course.

The original *Alexander von Humboldt* with her distinctive green sails.

Amerigo Vespucci

Italian Ship (fully rigged ship)

Website: www.marina.difesa.it

Crew	Cadets/Trainees	POR	Type	LOA
278	200	La Spezia	New build	102.38m

STS *Amerigo Vespucci* is owned and operated by the Italian Navy. She was launched in 1931 as one of a pair of training ships built to maintain traditional standards in the Naval Academy Cadets' military education and training. The other vessel, *Cristoforo Colombo*, was surrendered to the Soviet Union as war reparation after the Second World War, and renamed *Dunay*, although subsequently decommissioned.

Amerigo Vespucci's hull is steel but she was built to resemble a wooden warship of the early nineteenth century. Although not a warship, she does carry two six-powder saluting guns in pivot mountings on the deck, forward of the mainmast.

In Italy, passenger ships traditionally yield to the *Vespucci* and salute, sounding the horn three times. She is the oldest vessel in service with the Italian Navy.

Tip: Her figurehead is a small model of Amerigo Vespucci, the Italian explorer, cartographer and navigator, and the hull is painted black with two white stripes imitating two gun decks.

'Bluff your way' fact: When carrying cadets, the ship is usually steered from the manual stern rudder station, which is operated by four steering wheels with two men each. At other times, the hydraulically assisted steering on the bridge is used.

Amerigo Vespucci figurehead.

Capitan Miranda

Uruguayan three-masted Schooner

Website: www.capitanmiranda.org.uy

Crew	Cadets/Trainees	POR	Type	LOA
38	39	Montevideo	Restoration	60m

Capitan Miranda was originally built in Cadiz, Spain, in 1930 as a hydrographic vessel for the Uruguayan Navy. In 1976 there were plans to have her scrapped, but in 1978 a major refit was completed and she became a sail-training ship, acting as the school ship for the Uruguayan Navy. She is particularly colourful, with her decorated sails and gold figurehead reflecting the Uruguayan national symbol.

Although usually found in South American waters, in 1987 she sailed around the world and was one of a number of international ships that took part in the Australian bicentennial celebrations in Sydney. She has also taken part in several European and US tall ship races and festivals.

Tip: She carries the words 'Uruguay Natural' on her mainsails. Her nameplate can be found on her prow.

'Bluff your way' fact: In 2009 she won the prize for the ship furthest from home at the Funchal 500 Tall Ships regatta.

The prow carries the symbolic figurehead which was designed and produced by Uruguayan sculptors Andrés Santangello and Javier Abdala.

Christian Radich

Norwegian Ship (fully rigged ship)

Website: www.radich.no

Crew	Cadets/Trainees	POR	Type	LOA
15–20	80	Oslo	New build	73m

When merchant and captain Christian Radich from Oslo died in 1889, he left 90,000 Norwegian Kroner in his will to build a new school ship for Oslo. His only condition was that the ship should carry his name.

The current *Christian Radich* is the fourth ship to carry the name and was built in 1937 at Framnæs Yard, Sandefjord, as a sail-training vessel for the Norwegian Navy, but today it is operated by a foundation dedicated to preserving her for future generations.

The *Christian Radich* is one of only five square riggers that took part in the very first Tall Ships Race in 1956, coming second behind a British vessel called *Moyana*. She has been a regular competitor ever since, winning on many occasions, and fifty years on she won the fiftieth anniversary race, which was held over almost the same course. She carries five square sails on her foremast and main mast, and four on her mizzen.

She has made appearances in several films and on TV including the UK series *The Onedin Line* and the 1958 film *Windjammer*.

Fundraising to maintain Christian Radich is supported by the Friends (Venner) of Christian Radich, who have their own badge.

Tip: Look out for the distinctive gold scrollwork decoration on her bow beside the figurehead of a lady in a blue dress.

'Bluff your way' fact: One of the souvenirs sold to support the operation of the ship is a pair of socks embroidered with the words 'Christian Radich'.

Christian Radich under sail and, *below*, her figurehead..

Cisne Branco

Brazilian Ship (fully rigged ship)

Website: www.mar.mil.br

Crew	Cadets/Trainees	POR	Type	LOA
22	55	Rio de Janeiro	New build	88.4m

Cisne Branco (Portuguese for 'White Swan') was built in Amsterdam specifically for the Brazilian Navy; she was launched in 1999 and commissioned into the navy in 2000. Prior to this, the Brazilian Navy had operated two other tall ships, *Guanabra* (now *Sagres* of the Portuguese Navy) and *Almirante Saldanha*, but both were decommissioned in the 1960s.

Cisne Branco is used for training but also has a key role in enabling the Brazilian Navy to take part in festivals and races at home and abroad. She regularly attends Tall Ships Races in Europe and often can be distinguished by her large 'battle flag' – an oversized Brazilian national flag. Her nameplate is on her stern.

Tip: As a fully rigged ship she has square sails on all masts, but is unusual (although not unique) in having six yards on her main mast, five on her foremast and four on her mizzen. Her sister ship, *Stad Amsterdam* from the Netherlands, has the same sail plan, but it is easy to tell the difference as *Stad Amsterdam* has a black hull.

'Bluff your way' fact: The *Cisne Branco* is the third Brazilian Navy sail-training vessel to carry this name. The first *Cisne Branco* was a classic 15-metre wooden yacht, *Tritonia*, built in Scotland in 1910, which arrived in Brazil in 1978, when she was renamed. The second *Cisne Branco*, which had an aluminium hull, was used between 1980 and 1986, after which it was passed on to a naval college.

Cisne Branco with battle flag.

Cuauhtémoc

Mexican three-masted Barque

Crew	Cadets/Trainees	POR	Type	LOA
186	90	Acapulco	New build	89.72

Cuauhtémoc is owned by the Mexican Navy and is one of four ships built in Bilbao, Spain, in the early 1980s following a design originally used in the 1930s for the current *Gorch Fock*, from Germany. Her three sister ships, *Gloria*, *Guayas* and *Simon Bolivar*, are also all operated by South American navies.

She is renowned worldwide for her dramatic entry and exits to festivals, usually with her yards manned, and the sound of singing being broadcast out to spectators. She has won many prizes for 'the most spectacular entrance' to tall ship festivals and maritime events. Like many South American vessels she often can be seen with a battle flag as well (an oversized national flag flown from her stern).

Tip: Although her hull is white you will find her name written in green, as well as green trim near the bow and a green hull below the water line.

'Bluff your way' fact: *Cuauhtémoc* is named after an Aztec ruler of 1520, who is also represented in her figurehead. The name means 'one that has descended like an eagle'.

Opposite, left: *Cuauhtémoc*'s distinctive figurehead.

Opposite, right: Under full sail with *Sedov* in the background (before her hull was repainted black).

With yards manned.

Danmark

Danish Ship (fully rigged ship)

Website: https://www.martec.nu/en/trainingship-danmark.aspx

Crew	Cadets/Trainees	POR	Type	LOA
15	80	Copenhagen	New build	77m

The *Danmark* has had a fascinating history. Her predecessor, the tall ship *København* (Copenhagen), was lost at sea in 1928/1929.

Danmark was launched in 1933 to train Danish Merchant Navy personnel, and was in New York to participate in the 1939 World's Fair when the Second World War broke out. She was ordered to remain in US waters to avoid capture by the Germans, and moved to Jacksonville, Florida, where she was maintained with the help of the local Danish-American community. After the attack on Pearl Harbor, the captain, Knud Hansen, offered the ship to the US government as a training vessel. This offer was accepted, and the *Danmark* moved to Connecticut to train cadets at the United States Coastguard Academy.

In the 1970s she was one of seven tall ships used to film the BBC series *The Onedin Line*.

Tip: Her name, shown on the stern, has the Danish Royal Crown above in gold. Her home port is shown in Danish as København.

'Bluff your way' fact: She was originally designed for a crew of 120, but this was changed to eighty after a refit in 1959. The trainee sailors, but not the permanent crew, are still accommodated in hammocks.

Danmark under sail.

Danmark's figurehead, a golden representation of Neptune (shown here in front of the Polish ship *Dar Młodzieży*).

Dar Młodzieży

Polish Ship (fully rigged ship)

Crew	Cadets/Trainees	POR	Type	LOA
40	136	Gdynia	New build	108.8m

Dar Młodzieży, which means 'The Gift of Youth', was commissioned in 1982, the first of five sister ships built in Gdansk in the 1980s, and is used as a Maritime Academy training vessel. Her sister ships are *Mir*, *Druzhba*, *Pallada*, *Khersones* and *Nadezhda*. Her predecessor, *Dar Pormoza*, is now a museum ship in the port of Gdynia.

She was one of a number of European vessels that took part in the bicentennial celebrations in Australia in 1988. These days she is a regular at the European Tall Ships Races.

Tip: The Polish Ensign shows the national coat of arms, which is also displayed on the stern of the ship above her name. Unusually she carries her name on her bow as well.

'Bluff your way' fact: Under sail she can reach 16.5 knots compared to a maximum of 12 knots under engine power.

Dar Młodzieży in Aarhus 2013.

Dar Młodzieży alongside her sister ship *Mir* from Russia.

Dewaruci

Indonesian Barquentine

Crew	Cadets/Trainees	POR	Type	LOA
82	98	Surabaya	New build	58.3m

Dewaruci was built in Germany by H. C. Stülcken & Sohn, with work beginning on her in 1932. Shortly after the outbreak of the Second World War, the shipyard sustained heavy damage and work stopped. She was finally completed in 1952 and launched in 1953. Since then, she has been based out of Surabaya on the Java Sea. Her name and figurehead represent the Javanese wayang (puppet theatre) god of truth and courage.

During her travels around the world, in addition to being a naval training ship, she helps to promote tourism to her home country with the tag line, 'Wonderful Indonesia'.

Due to her age, *Dewaruci* is expected to be retired in 2014 and will probably be an exhibit in the Indonesian maritime museum. The Indonesian parliament has commissioned a new tall ship and has set aside $80 million (Rp720 billion) for the purpose. The new ship, a Barque, will be built in Vigo, Spain, and will also be named *Dewaruci*; she is expected to be completed in 2014/2015.

Tip: Although generally spelt *Dewaruci* (or sometimes *Dewa Ruci*), the ship's bell carries the name *Dewarutji*.

'Bluff your way' fact: The masts are named after the three sons of King Pandu, from the Sanskrit legends. The foremast is named 'Bima', the mainmast is 'Arjuna' and the mizzenmast 'Yudhistira'.

Dewaruci in New York, dressed overall and with her yards manned.

Dewaruci figurehead.

Dewaruci ship's bell.

Eagle

American three-masted Barque

Website: www.uscga.edu/eagle

Crew	Cadets/Trainees	POR	Type	LOA
61	150	New London, USA	Restoration	90m

USCGC *Eagle* was built in 1936, originally as the SSS *Horst Wessel*, the flagship of the Kriegsmarine (German Navy) sail-training fleet, which included the original *Gorch Fock* (now a museum ship) and the *Albert Leo Schlageter* (now the Portuguese ship *Sagres III*).

Horst Wessel was decommissioned in 1939 with the onset of the Second World War but recommissioned in late 1942. At the end of the war she was one of several vessels distributed to various nations as war reparations. The ship was taken by the United States and was commissioned into the United States Coastguard as the Coastguard Cutter *Eagle* on 15 May 1946.

She occasionally takes part in the European Tall Ships Races and was one of a number of international vessels that sailed to Australia for the bicentennial celebrations in 1988.

Tip: Her distinctive red band (racing stripe) is the same as seen on most coastguard vessels and aircraft from around the world.

'Bluff your way' fact: Rudolf Hess gave the speech at her launch in the presence of Adolf Hitler.

Her triple helm allows six people to steer in heavy weather.

Seen here as the SSS (Segelschulschiffe) *Horst Wessel*.

Eendracht

Dutch Schooner

Website: www.eendracht.nl

Crew	Cadets/Trainees	POR	Type	LOA
13+	38	Rotterdam	New build	58.8m

Launched in 1989, *Eendracht* has been a regular participant in the Tall Ships Races ever since, winning many prizes and awards.

She is operated by a not-for-profit Dutch foundation. Although youngsters up to the age of twenty-five have precedence, anyone can book to sail. The *Eendracht* also organises school trips and special trips for those youths with the risk of being left out. Stimulation, working together, discipline, team spirit and perseverance play a large role in all of this. Whenever possible, ill children are also given these opportunities and the foundation works closely with local hospitals to make this possible.

Tip: *Eendracht* is gaff rigged on the foremast and mainmast.

'Bluff your way' fact: The majority of the professional crew are volunteers and the organisation has over 300 on the books, from captains to boatswains (bosuns or, to be correct, bo's'ns) and doctors.

Above: Dressed overall in Aarhus, 2013.

Right: Eendracht under sail.

Europa

Dutch Barque

Website: www.barkeuropa.com

Crew	Cadets/Trainees	POR	Type	LOA
15	48	Amsterdam	Restoration	56m

Europa was built in 1911 at the Stülcken shipyard in Hamburg, Germany, and originally named *Senator Brockes*. The ship was put into service as lightship *Elbe 4* on the River Elbe, and later worked as a stand-by vessel. In 1986 the ship was brought to the Netherlands and, over a period of eight years, was completely rebuilt and rigged as a Barque.

She is now operated as a sail-training vessel, and people of all ages and backgrounds can sail on her. The working language on board is English.

She regularly visits Antarctica during the Northern Hemisphere winter, and takes part in the Tall Ships Races in the European summer. She was also one of three Dutch vessels that circumnavigated the globe to join the tall ships festivals and International Fleet Review in Australia in 2013.

Tip: Her figurehead is easily recognised as a naked woman (the mortal woman Europa) reaching for a white bull (representing the Greek God Zeus).

'Bluff your way' fact: The current figurehead was fitted in 2010 after the previous one was damaged and lost due to contact with an iceberg in Antarctica.

Europa's figurehead.

Europa in the ice (with her old figurehead).

Europa showing her unusual 'studding sails' or stud'sails.

Georg Stage

Danish Ship (fully rigged ship)

Website: www.georgstage.dk

Crew	Cadets/Trainees	POR	Type	LOA
10	63	Copenhagen	New build	54m

The *Georg Stage* is operated by the Georg Stage Memorial Foundation, and is used as a training ship for both prospective merchant seamen and cadets from the Royal Danish Navy. During the time on board, young people aged between seventeen and twenty can gain the qualifications required to join a commercial vessel as seamen or chefs.

The trainees still sleep in hammocks, boys and girls alongside each other, although they do shower at different times!

She was built in just five months in 1934 and started training in April 1935. *Georg Stage* was one of the ships that took part in the very first Tall Ships Race in 1956 and came second in Class A in the fiftieth anniversary race held in 2006, beaten by another contestant from 1956, *Christian Radich*.

Tip: She has a distinctive gold band around the top of her dark hull.

'Bluff your way' fact: Her figurehead was transferred from an earlier ship of the same name launched in 1882. It portrays Georg Stage, who was the son of the original shipowner and died of tuberculosis at the age of twenty-two.

Above: Under sail.

Right: *Georg Stage* figurehead.

Below: *Georg Stage* with *Gulden Leeuw*.

ARC *Gloria*

Colombian Barque

Crew	Cadets/Trainees	POR	Type	LOA
56	120	Cartagena, Colombia	New build	65.6m

Armada Nacional República de Colombia (ARC) is the Spanish name for the navy (armada) of Columbia, and the initials ARC are used both as an abbreviation for the navy and as a prefix for their ships.

Gloria was built in 1968 as a sail-training ship for the Columbian navy following a long campaign by one of the senior admirals at the time. He eventually extracted a promise from the defence minister at a social function, and he gave the admiral a napkin, with the pledge 'Vale por un velero' ('Valid for one sailing ship') written on it. She is now the navy's official flagship.

She is named after the words of the Columbian national anthem, 'Oh Gloria inmarcesible', which translates as 'Oh Unfading Glory'.

Tip: When manning the yards on ceremonial occasions, the crew of *Gloria* wear red, blue and yellow clothes to mirror the colours of the Columbian national flag.

'Bluff your way' fact: Every step on the ship has the name 'Gloria' embedded in the solid brass scuff-plates.

Above: *Gloria* with yards manned and battle flag flying.

Right: *Gloria*'s figurehead, an angel coated in gold-leaf, is called Maria Salud, believed to be the name of the sculptor's daughter.

Gorch Fock

German Barque

Website: www.marine.de/portal/a/marine

Crew	Cadets/Trainees	POR	Type	LOA
85	138	Kiel	New build	89.2m

The first ship called *Gorch Fock* was built for the German navy in 1933; after a chequered history, she ended up as a museum ship. This first *Gorch Fock* was a vessel of a similar design to the USCGC *Eagle*, which is still sailing.

At the end of the Second World War, Germany lost all its training ships as part of the war reparation. The current *Gorch Fock* was commissioned in 1958, based on broadly the same design as the original, although some late changes were made following the sinking of *Pamir* in 1957. She is a training ship for officers and NCOs of the German navy. As her home port is Kiel, the tops of her fore and main masts can be lowered so that she can navigate the Kiel Canal, otherwise she would not be able to pass under some of the bridges.

Tip: Look out for her relatively short bowsprit and light-coloured masts and yards.

'Bluff your way' fact: The ship appeared on a 1960 version of the 10 Deutsche Mark note.

Above left: *Gorch Fock* on the 1960 10 Deutsche Mark note.

Above right: *Gorch Fock*'s figurehead, a stylised Albatross, shown here with *Dar Młodzieży* in the background.

      Tall Ships Handbook

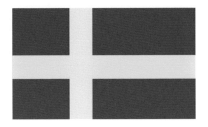 

Götheborg

Swedish Ship (fully rigged ship)

Crew	Cadets/Trainees	POR	Type	LOA
20	60	Gothenburg	Replica	58m

The current ship is a replica of the original *Götheborg*, which sank after running aground in Gothenburg harbour in 1745. She was built over a period of ten years to be as close as possible to the original design. This was achieved after extensive research, including diving on the wreck, as there were no original drawings available. She is almost certainly the largest operational wooden sailing ship in the world, being 58 metres in length. She began sailing in 2005 with an eighteen-month trip to China, which was the regular destination of the original ship.

She often takes part in the maritime festivals and Tall Ships Races, and has a world tour planned for 2020. Berths for trainees, referred to as deckhands, are open to people of all backgrounds and there are also opportunities to help with maintenance as a volunteer.

She carries cannon on board which can be fired on ceremonial occasions.

Tip: She can be easily identified by her large golden lion figurehead and decorative stern.

'Bluff your way' fact: As a historical replica, *Götheborg* is allowed to fly the two-tongued flag of the Swedish East India Company rather than a current flag or ensign.

Under sail showing her studding sails (stud'sails) used in light winds.

Above left: *Götheborg*'s figurehead.

Above right: Decorative stern and East India flag.

Grossherzogin Elisabeth

German Schooner

Crew	Cadets/Trainees	POR	Type	LOA
8	50	Elsfleth	Restoration	63.7m

Grossherzogin Elisabeth is a 1909 German sailing ship built as the *San Antonio*, a replacement for the 1907 freighter *San Antonio*, which was lost following a collision at sea in 1908.

In 1914, the new *San Antonio* ran aground off the coast of Morocco, and in 1929 she capsized near Copenhagen. However, she was salvageable and was converted into a coastal trading vessel. Her next lease of life was as the cruise ship *Ariadne*.

In 1982, the ship was sold and a sail-training club was founded to operate her as the *Grossherzogin Elisabeth*. She is affectionately known as the 'Lissi'.

Although she is primarily used for sail training and runs a four-week training trip for interns in Nautical Studies once a year, in the Easter and autumn holidays there are courses run in conjunction with the University of Applied Sciences in Wilhelmshaven and the Department of Maritime Studies in Elsfleth.

In the summer season day trips are conducted over the weekends, and during the summer holidays *Lissi* takes part whenever she can in regattas and tall ship festivals and races.

Note: The *Duchesse Anne*, a French fully rigged ship formerly known as *Grossherzogin Elisabeth*, built in 1901, is now moored permanently in Dunkirk.

Tip: her name can be found in blue on her stern and also on her bow. She carries a matching blue line along her hull.

'Bluff your way' fact: Her figurehead represents Duchess Elisabeth Alexandrin of Mecklenburg-Schwerin, who died in September 1955 at the age of eighty-six and for whom the ship is named.

Stern view.

Under sail. Picture: Courtesy VollertBIT

Guayas

Ecuadorean Barque

Crew	Cadets/Trainees	POR	Type	LOA
155	80	Quito	New build	79.5m

Guayas is one of four similar sailing ships that were built in Bilbao, *Gloria* (Colombia) being the closest in design to *Guayas*. The other two sister ships are *Simón Bolívar* (Venezuela), and *Cuauhtémoc* (Mexico). These four ships are broadly based on *Gorch Fock*, which was built more than four decades earlier.

She was built as the training ship for the Armada del Ecuador, the Ecuadorean navy.

Guayas was named after the river on which the Ecuadorean Naval School is situated, and she has been providing sail training for cadets from this college since she was launched in 1976.

Tip: Her name is on her stern, surrounded by a gold wreath of leaves; her figurehead is a Condor.

'Bluff your way' fact: On her first visit to Asia, she took on a sailor from the Chinese navy as a trainee to learn about square-rigged sailing.

As a training vessel, traditional knotting and rope work is a key part of life on board and are often on show in port.

Her life rings show her as a 'Buque Escuela' or 'School ship'.

Condor on bow of *Guayas*.

Like many of the South American tall ships *Guayas* carries an oversized 'battle flag' for entry and exit to festival ports.

Gulden Leeuw

Dutch three-masted Topsail Schooner

Website: www.guldenleeuw.com

Crew	Cadets/Trainees	POR	Type	LOA
14	80	Rotterdam	Restoration	70.1m

The *Gulden Leeuw* was originally built in 1937 as the *Dana*, a research vessel for the Danish government. In 2009 the *Dana* was converted into *Gulden Leeuw*, one of the largest three masted Topsail Schooners in the world. During the conversion, many of her original features were retained, and as well as the large middle deck there is a captain's VIP lounge with Chesterfield sofas.

    The *Gulden Leeuw* offers a range of sail-training voyages for all ages. In 2013, she received the award for the most innovative initiative – awarded to the sail-training ship that had developed its own version of a sail-training programme. The working language on board is English, meaning that trainees come from all over Europe to sail on her.

Tip: Although as a Topsail Schooner she would usually be a Class B, at a little over 70 m *Gulden Leeuw* is longer than many of the Class A vessels.

'Bluff your way' fact: *Gulden Leeuw* is owned by two married couples who operate the charters under the name 'P & T Charters'.

Gulden Leeuw under sail.

Gulden Leeuw, Wylde Swan and *Sørlandet* during the 2011 Tall Ships Races.

VIP lounge *Gulden Leeuw*.

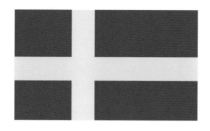 

Gunilla

Swedish Barque

Website: www.add-maritime.se

Crew	Cadets/Trainees	POR	Type	LOA
11	44	Öckerö	Restoration	61.44m

Gunilla was built as a motorsailor in the late 1930s, and from 1940 was used as a cargo vessel. Between 1997 and 1999 she was rebuilt into a three-masted Barque and given a new figurehead of a young woman modelled after Gunilla, the daughter of a former owner; the original is in the maritime museum of Oskarshamn. She was also given a new ship's bell by the 'Friends of Gunilla' in 2012.

Since 1999 she has been active as sailing college Den Seglande Gymnasieskolan (Sailing Upper-Secondary School), where social studies and maritime students between the ages of sixteen and nineteen spend about sixty days on board as part of their education.

She undertakes a regular programme of five voyages a year, which form part of the fixed syllabus for students:

Öckerö (Sweden) down to Cadiz (Spain) via Germany, France, England and Ireland.
Cadiz to Gibraltar, Minorca, Corsica and Barcelona then repositions in Malaga.
Malaga (Spain) to Miami (the US) via Morocco, Cape Verde, Grenada and the Dominican Republic.
Then to and from Miami (the US) sailing to Cuba, Belize and Mexico.
And finally from Miami home to Öckerö (Sweden), via South Carolina, Bermuda, the Azores and France.

Tip: Her name is in black script on her stern.

'Bluff your way' fact: Although she was named *Gunilla* when launched as a cargo ship and sails under that name today, for a short period from 1961 to 1965 she was renamed *Monica*.

Above: Gunilla under sail.

Right: Gunilla's name on her stern.

Iskra

Polish Barquentine

Website: www.orpiskra.info (this is an unofficial website, not the Polish Navy site)

Crew	Cadets/Trainees	POR	Type	LOA
18	45	Gdynia	New build	49m

Commissioned in 1982, *Iskra* (meaning Spark) is the second of three sister ships built in Gdansk; the first was another Polish vessel, *Pogoria,* and the third the Bulgarian Barquentine *Kaliakra.* Iskra is the second sailing ship in the Polish Navy to have this name. The first was a wooden, three-masted gaff Schooner, which sailed under the Polish Navy ensign for fifty years between 1927 and 1977.

In addition to acting as a training ship for the Polish Navy, during the summer she takes young people from youth organisations on sail-training voyages, participating in festivals and Tall Ships Races in Europe and wider afield. In 1996 she became the first Polish ship to circumnavigate the globe.

Tip: Her hull, with its red stripe on white, represents the Polish national colours.

'Bluff your way' fact: Often referred to as ORP *Iskra*, the letters ORP should be said individually, not pronounced as a word. They are the equivalent to the British HMS (Her Majesty's Ship) and are an abbreviation for 'Ship of the Republic of Poland' in Polish.

Iskra under sail.

Iskra alongside with *Dar Młodzieży* in Aarhus showing the relative sizes (49 m and 108.8 m).

Jeanie Johnston

Irish Barque

Website: www.jeaniejohnston.ie

Crew	Cadets/Trainees	POR	Type	LOA
11	29	Tralee	Replica	47m

The current *Jeanie Johnston* was built at Blennerville, Tralee, Ireland, as a replica of a Barque built by John Munn at Quebec in 1847. After the Great Famine in Ireland, during which a million people died of hunger and another million emigrated, the original *Jeanie Johnston* carried starving emigrants from Blennerville to the New World, bringing timber back to Europe on return trips.

The replica was built to commemorate the 150th anniversary of the famine and as a millennium project to celebrate the historic links between Ireland and North America. In the first few years after she was completed, she carried out several sail-training voyages, including visits to the USA and Canada, and took part in the 2005 Tall Ships Race. Sadly, since 2010 she has not been deemed seaworthy and is now a museum ship in Dublin. However, there are plans for her to be used for day sails, which may lead to a new lease of life at sea.

Tip: She can be found at Custom House Quay in Dublin.

'Bluff your way' fact: Between 1848 and 1855, the original *Jeanie Johnston* carried over 2,500 emigrants on seven-week voyages to the New World, and no life was ever lost on board.

Jeanie Johnston (black and white hull) with Irish Sail Training ship *Asgard* (since lost at sea).

Jeanie Johnston figurehead of unnamed woman.

Kaliakra

Bulgarian Barquentine

Website: www.kaliakra.bmtc-bg.com

Crew	Cadets/Trainees	POR	Type	LOA
13	36	Varna	New build	52m

Kaliakra was built in Gdansk in 1984 as one of three sister ships. The other two are the Polish ships ORP *Iskra* and *Pogoria*, both of which are still sailing.

The ship is owned and operated by the Bulgarian Maritime Training Centre. The ship was specially designed for the training and qualification of students from the Maritime Academy in Varna – the future officers of the Bulgarian merchant fleet.

However, she also offers sail-training voyages to young people over the age of ten and adults with no maximum age, who can join for some voyages during the summer. Historically she has taken part in many Tall Ships Races and festivals, although she missed 2012.

Figurehead, pictured in Istanbul with the Blue Mosque in the background.

Tip: Her name and port of registration appear on the stern in Cyrillic script.

'Bluff your way' fact: Her figurehead represents a young Bulgarian girl, one of forty who, according to legend, threw themselves off the headland known as Kaliakra rather than be captured by the Ottomans.

Above left: *Kaliakra* under sail

Above right: Stern showing her name and Port of Registration in Cyrillic.

Kaliakra in heavy seas.

Khersones

Ukrainian Ship (three-masted fully rigged ship)

Crew	Cadets/Trainees	POR	Type	LOA
42	72–91	Kerch	New build	108.8m

Khersones is one of six sister ships built at the Gdansk shipyard in Poland in the 1980s. She is named after the city of Kherson in Ukraine. Two of the others of the same design, the Russian *Mir* and the Polish *Dar Młodzieży*, are still regular competitors in the Tall Ships Races. Until 2011 Khersones also took part but she is currently laid up, with an unknown future.

From 1991, the Ukrainian *Khersones* was used as a sail-training ship for cadets and also offered berths, with the option to join as a sail-training trainee or a passenger

Tip: She is easily identified by her red hull.

'Bluff your way' fact: The six sisters are *Mir*, *Dar Młodzieży*, *Druzhba*, *Pallada*, *Khersones* and *Nadezhda*.

Parade of Sail with *Khersones* and *Mir* nearest to camera.

Khersones under sail.

Bowsprit showing part of her name in Cyrillic script.

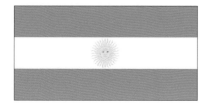

Libertad

Argentinian Ship (three-masted fully rigged ship)

Website: www.ara.mil.ar

Crew	Cadets/Trainees	POR	Type	LOA
211	150	Buenos Aires	New build	103.6m

Originally ordered by the Argentinean Navy in 1953 to be their school (training) ship, *Libertad* was eventually commissioned ten years later in 1963. Her midlife update between 2004 and 2007 is expected to extend her life for another forty years.

She carries four fully functioning cannon, used only on ceremonial occasions. She takes part in races and festivals throughout the world, appearing in European and US Tall Ships races, the Australian bicentennial celebrations and the South American tall ship regattas in 2010 and 2014.

Above left: *Libertad* stern.

Above right: Figurehead.

Tip: Her wood-carved figurehead represents Liberty in a long flowing robe, and her stern holds the Argentine coat of arms in bronze.

'Bluff your way' fact: In October 2012 *Libertad* was siezed and impounded in Ghana, as a result of a court ruling in favour of NML Capital, part of a Cayman Islands hedge fund, which claimed that it was owed US $370 million as a consequence of Argentina's debt defaults of 2002. Eventually the UN ruled that, as a military ship, she had immunity, and she was released.

Above: Libertad with neatly furled sails.

Right: Under sail.

Loa

Danish Barquentine

Website: www.loa.dk

Crew	Cadets/Trainees	POR	Type	LOA
8	26	Aalborg	Restoration	38.8m

Loa was originally built as the three-masted Schooner *Aphrodite* in Svendborg, Denmark, in 1922. She was restored as a Barquentine in Aalborg and relaunched in 2007.

One of three Danish Class A ships (along with *Danmark* and *Georg Stage*) the vessel is now owned by the Danish sail-training trust, the Tall Ship Aalborg Fund. Berths are available on board for young people over the age of fifteen, either for personal development and sail training or as an introduction to a maritime career. She is a frequent competitor in Tall Ships Races, particularly when held in her home waters.

When the STI International Tall Ship Conference was held in her home port of Aalborg in 2013, *Loa* was alongside to welcome delegates from around the world.

Tip: Her traditional lines and lack of obvious superstructure distinguish her from other similar vessels.

'Bluff your way' fact: Originally named *Aphrodite*, she has also been called *Johanne* and *Dorrit*, but was renamed *Loa* in 1952.

Loa under sail.

Crew of *Loa* in Antwerp as part of
Tall Ships Race crew parade.

Lord Nelson

British Barque

Website: www.jst.org.uk

Crew	Cadets/Voyage Crew	POR	Type	LOA
8	38	Southampton	New build	55m

Lord Nelson was commissioned by the Jubilee Sailing Trust to be the 'flagship' for their mission to integrate able-bodied and disabled people using the sail-training experience on board. Early trials aboard the Barque *Marques*, the Brig *Royalist* and subsequently the Brigantine *Soren Larsen* enabled Colin Mudie to design a ship that would meet the rather unusual requirements.

Work began in 1984 when enough funds had been raised to enable a start on the building of Colin Mudie's design No. 342, *Lord Nelson*, and she was launched in 1986. She sails with trainees (known as voyage crew) made up of up to 50 per cent people with physical disabilities and 50 per cent able-bodied people. *Lord Nelson* and the JST's second ship, *Tenacious*, are the only two ships of their kind in the world. Berths are available to people aged sixteen and over, of any nationality, with no upper age limit.

Lord Nelson usually takes part in the European Tall Ships Races, but between 2012 and 2014 circumnavigated the globe, taking her message to every continent of the world.

Tip: Her bowsprit is designed to enable wheelchair users access, and therefore does not look as traditional as other vessels.

'Bluff your way' fact: *Lord Nelson* has two sister ships broadly based on the same design by Colin Mudie, both operated by the Indian Navy: *Tarangini* commissioned in 1997 and *Sudarshini* commissioned in 2012.

Voyage crew on the bowsprit.

Loth Loriën

Dutch Barquentine

Website: www.restchart.com

Crew	Cadets/Trainees	POR	Type	LOA
3	36	Amsterdam	Restoration	48m

The *Loth Loriën* has had an eventful history. Originally built in Bergen in 1907, she sailed as the herring lugger *Njord*. Around 1992 she was converted into a two-masted lugger with modern rigging and provided with a modern interior. In 2002, the ship was again modernised and refitted and put to sea as a three-masted fore-and-aft Schooner.

More recently, in 2009 the ship was re-rigged again, this time as a Barquentine. Although she can be found as part of the Tall Ships Races and it is possible to get an individual berth, the majority of her time is spent on corporate and group charters, and she offers kitesurfing and other adventurous activities alongside the sailing. She is privately owned by the same family as the *J R Tolkien*, and the name *Loth Loriën* also has a Tolkien connection, as it was the name of a forest located in Middle Earth in *The Lord of the Rings*.

Tip: Her name appears clearly in black lower-case lettering along her white bow.

'Bluff your way' fact: At one stage *Loth Loriën* had an onboard open-air Jacuzzi.

Loth Lorien as a Schooner.

With her current sailplan as a Barquentine.

Mir

Russian Ship (fully rigged ship)

Website: www.tallshipmir.com

Crew	Cadets/Trainees	POR	Type	LOA
55	144	St Petersburg	New build	109.2m

Mir (meaning Peace in Russian) was the second of the six Gdansk sister ships to be built. The others are *Dar Młodzieży, Druzhba, Pallada, Khersones* and *Nadezhda*. Her website offers several excellent options for interactive on-board tours with high-resolution images taken from different vantage points on board; although it is in Russian, it is fairly easy to navigate through the graphics.

Her name, 'Мир', and port of registration, 'Санкт-Петербург', are on her stern in Cyrillic (see picture with *Dar Młodzieży* on her page). She is owned by the Admiral Makarov State Maritime Academy (AMSMA) and is used as its main training vessel. However, she does sell berths to members of the public and there are often opportunities to sail on her in Tall Ship Races, mainly in Europe

Tip: *Mir*'s distinctive blue strip on a white hull distinguishes her from her five sister ships, and her image is often used to represent sail-training events even when she is not part of the fleet.

'Bluff your way' fact: Although she has a full complement of 199, she can be sailed with just thirty people.

Mir leaves Aarhus during the 2013 Tall Ships Races.

Under full sail.

Mircea

Romanian Barque

Website: www.anmb.ro

Crew	Cadets/Trainees	POR	Type	LOA
80	120	Constanta	New build	82.1m

Mircea is one of a series of ships built in Hamburg in the 1930s, which include *Eagle*, *Sagres* and *Gorch Fock*. The name comes from Mircea the Old, who led Romania from 1386 to 1418, and the crowned figurehead shows his image with distinctive blue shirt and red-and-white flowing robes.

Although she has crossed the Atlantic on three occasions, her main sailing area is closer to home in the Mediterranean and Black Sea. She takes part in the Tall Ship Races and festivals when they are held in her home area. She is one of two training ships operated by the Romanian Naval Academy, although the only sailing ship.

Tip: Look for her bright golden yellow topline.

'Bluff your way' fact: In September 1944, during the Second World War, *Mircea*, along with several other Romanian vessels, was captured by the Soviets and sent to join the Russian fleet in the Black Sea. After the war, the Romanian authorities successfully negotiated for its return and it rejoined the Romanian fleet in May 1946.

Above: Under sail.

Right: Mircea's figurehead.

Nadezhda

Russian Ship (fully rigged ship)

Website: www.msun.ru

Crew	Cadets/Trainees	POR	Type	LOA
79	120	Vladivostok	New build	108.8m

Nadezhda is perhaps less well known than some of her five famous sisters: *Dar Młodzieży, Druzhba, Pallada, Khersones* and *Mir.*

She is operated by the Russian Far East State Maritime Academy, which is the centre of marine education and training in the far east of Russia. It provides maritime education and training for specialists in technical, natural science and humanitarian areas. Her name, like other Russian ships, appears in Cyrillic script: Надежда.

Although the vessel entry list for Tall Ship Races frequently shows a Russian vessel called *Nadezhda*, this is often the smaller Class B vessel of the same name. However, the Class A *Nadezhda* has taken part herself, and is scheduled to appear in the 2014 race in the Black Sea area.

Tip: Her foremast often carries a sail showing the coat of arms of the Russian Federation.

'Bluff your way' fact: The name *Nadezhda* (which is Russian for Hope) is a traditional name for ships in the Russian fleet. The first ever ship to bear the name was built in 1728.

Under light sail.

The Russian schooner *Nadezhda*, a Class B vessel of the same name.

Coat of arms as displayed.

Oosterschelde

Dutch three-masted Topsail Schooner

Website: www.oosterschelde.nl

Crew	Cadets/Trainees	POR	Type	LOA
7	24	Rotterdam	Restoration	50m

Three-masted Topsail Schooner *Oosterschelde* is the largest restored Dutch sailing ship. As a Topsail Schooner, she is categorised as a Class A vessel by virtue of her length (over 40 m). The ship was built as a freighter for transatlantic trade in 1917, carrying a variety of cargo. After a considerable restoration between 1988 and 1992, the ship now primarily operates as a sail-training vessel, but is also well appointed for corporate entertaining. She takes paying trainees year round, including on her Antarctica voyages.

She is one of three Dutch ships, along with *Europa* and the Class B vessel *Tecla*, that circumnavigated the world between 2012 and 2014 and joined the International Fleet Review celebrating the Royal Australian Navy centenary in Sydney. For *Oosterschelde* this was her second time around the world.

Tip: She has broad white flashes on the bow and stern which do not meet midships.

'Bluff your way' fact: She has a piano on board in the main salon.

Oosterschelde in Antarctica.

Oosterschelde under sail.

Oosterschelde's well-appointed salon.

Pallada

Russian Ship (fully rigged ship)

Website: www.dalrybvtuz.ru/pallada

Crew	Cadets/Trainees	POR	Type	LOA
80	120	Vladivostock	New build	109.2

Pallada is one of the six famous sisters built in Gdansk in the 1980s, along with *Mir*, *Kherzones*, *Dar Młodzieży*, *Druzhba* and *Nadezhda*.

Although her name appears in Cyrillic as Паллада, when in port she usually displays name board and banners with her name shown as *Pallada*. She is operated by the Russian Far Eastern Technical Fisheries University as a training vessel and, like *Nadezhda*, is registered in Vladivostock. Each year local high school students are invited to open days to prepare for joining her training schemes. During her worldwide travels she operates exchanges with other maritime training establishments.

Tip: She is the only one of the six ships of her design to have a paint scheme imitating the old gun ports. Vessels with similar schemes include the British vessel *Royalist* and the Pakistani Navy ship *Rah Naward* (previously the *Prince William*).

'Bluff your way' fact: *Pallada* claims to hold the world record for the fastest Class A ship under sail, officially registered at 18.7 knots in 2009.

View of *Pallada*'s bow, alongside.

Pallada with her fore mast and mizzen mast yards manned.

Cadets on board *Pallada*.

Pelican of London

British Mainmast Barquentine

Website: www.adventureundersail.com

Crew	Cadets/Trainees	POR	Type	LOA
11	28	London	Restoration	45m

Pelican (her original name) was built in Le Havre, France, in 1948 and was sold to work in Norway as an Arctic fishing trawler, where she remained until 1968 when she became a coaster and was renamed *Kadett*.

In 1995, work began to transform her into a tall ship, and was completed in 2007. She is often called by the full name *Pelican of London* as shown on her stern, although she is based out of Weymouth. Although privately owned, she offers sail-training berths during Tall Ships Races, and the berths are operated through the charity Adventure under Sail.

At the beginning and end of the season she operates a number of day sails, but during the summer generally takes part in the Tall Ships Races and festivals. In the winter she can sometimes be found in the Caribbean or other warmer waters.

Tip: Although classified as a Barquentine, it is her main (middle) mast that is square rigged rather than the more usual fore mast.

'Bluff your way' fact: Because of her unique sail plan she is sometimes referred to as a mainmast Barquentine.

Above left: Stern view.

Above right: Under sail.

Above: Pelican's figurehead.

Right: Pelican at sea in choppy weather.

Picton Castle

Cook Islands-registered, Canadian-based Barque

Website: www.picton-castle.com

Crew	Cadets/Trainees	POR	Type	LOA
12	40	Avatiu	Restoration	57.06m

Picton Castle was a minesweeper in the British Royal Navy during the Second World War. In 1955, she was sold to Norwegian owners and overhauled to be powered by a diesel engine and other auxiliary engines. Under the name *Dolmar*, she freighted up and down the Norwegian coast until she was taken out of service in the late 1980s, when the success of the railways made her uneconomical.

In 1996/1997, she was taken to Lunenburg, Nova Scotia, home of the traditional Canadian fishing Schooner fleet, to be overhauled and fitted as a sailing vessel. Although she sails worldwide and is registered in the Cook Islands, Lunenburg is still her home port. She is a sail-training vessel, and still regularly carries essential cargo, supplies and educational materials to far-flung islands in the South Pacific.

Although shorter legs are available, the intention is for trainees to join for up to ten months and complete long ocean passages. A typical voyage would be from Fiji, across the Pacific, through the Caribbean, finishing in the USA or Canada. As a result she is not often seen at festivals or taking part in Tall Ship Races.

Tip: A distinguishing feature is her mustard-coloured deckhouse towards the stern.

'Bluff your way' fact: The *Picton Castle* has a ship's cat. The first cat, Chibley, had about 250,000 sea miles under her paws and sailed around the world five times. Her successor is called George.

Above left: The stern of *Picton Castle*.

Above right: Chibley, the first ship's cat.

Above left: And George keeping an eye on a fish.

Above right: *Picton Castle* under sail.

Pogoria

Polish Barquentine

Website: www.pogorial.pl

Crew	Cadets/Trainees	Port of Registration	Type	LOA
11	41	Gdynia	New build	47m

Like many tall ships, *Pogoria* was built in the Polish shipyards in Gdansk. Originally used by the marine educational project, the Iron Shackle Fraternity, she is now owned and operated by the Polish Sail Training Association. The Iron Shackle Fraternity was a group opposed to Soviet domination of Poland, and their symbol represented the repressive regime and was defiantly depicted on the sails of *Pogoria* in her early days; it is still portrayed on her bow today.

Nowadays *Pogoria* is dedicated to sail training, and most voyages are booked for groups rather than individuals. However, there are a number of opportunities each year to apply for individual berths. She is a regular participant in Tall Ships Races and festivals, particularly those held in the Baltic or North Sea areas.

Tip: Her hull has white paintwork with a wide dark-blue band from bow to stern. Her name appears along the bow and on her stern.

'Bluff your way' fact: In 2011, during the Tall Ships Race to St Petersburg, all three of her masts broke and the thirty-seven trainees were all airlifted ashore by two helicopters of the Finnish Boarder Guard; the ship was towed to port to be repaired.

Pogoria stern.

Pogoria closely followed by *Christian Radich* off Norway.

Royal Helena

Bulgarian Barquentine

Website: http://www.topsail.bg

Crew	Cadets/Trainees	POR	Type	LOA
9	47	Varna	New build	54.4m

One of the newer ships in the tall ship fleet, *Royal Helena* has already taken part in a number of events and her future programme shows that she is planning to appear in as many European races and festivals as possible. She was purpose built in Bulgaria as a sail-training vessel, and the majority of her trainees come from the Varna Maritime High School.

She is owned by the Bulgarian company Topsail Ltd, and as well as sail-training voyages she operates day sails for up to 100 passengers, and three-day passenger trips to Istanbul from her home port of Varna.

Her name Роял Хелена and port of registration Варна appear on her stern in Bulgarian (Cyrillic letters, as shown here).

Tip: Her masts and bowsprit are yellow, matching the yellow band on her black hull.

'Bluff your way' fact: Sometimes *Royal Helena* will carry both paying passengers and maritime cadets on the same trip, and has a few 'luxury' cabins on board as well as dormitories.

Royal Helena's figurehead.

Royal Helena in the Black Sea.

Sagres

Portuguese Barque

Website: www.marinha.pt

Crew	Cadets/Trainees	POR	Type	LOA
126	66	Lisbon	New build	89.5m

Originally built for the German Navy and called *Albert Leo Schlageter*, she was launched in 1937. She sustained considerable damage on her first training voyage in early 1938 as a result of a collision with a steam ship in dense fog in the Straits of Dover. She was damaged again in 1944 after hitting a submerged mine.

Her sister ship was given to the USA as part of war reparation and now sails as the US Coastguard vessel *Eagle*. *Sagres* was also originally destined for the USA but was eventually given to Brazil as recompense for the damage done to the Brazilian fleet. She became the training ship *Guanabara* until 1961 when she was sold to her current owners, the Portuguese Navy, for $150,000.

She is an occasional participant in the European Tall Ships Races.

Tip: Under sail she is easily identified by the Portuguese Crosses of Christ (sometimes known as Maltese crosses) on the squaresails. These have been used as symbols on Portuguese ships since the fourteenth century and appear in the coat of arms.

'Bluff your way' fact: She is named after the port of Sagres, which was the base for the famous fifteenth-century explorer, Prince Henry the Navigator. The figurehead is a bust of Prince Henry.

Sagres' figurehead.

Sagres stern view.

Sagres under sail.

Shabab Oman

Omani Barquentine

Crew	Cadets/Trainees	POR	Type	LOA
9	36	Muscat	New build	52.1m

The ship was originally built in 1971 as a Schooner for the Dulverton Trust as part of a UK youth programme. She was sold to the Sultanate of Oman in 1977, re-rigged as a Barquentine and named *Shabab Oman*, which means 'Youth of Oman'. For a while she was maintained by the Ministry for Youth but was transferred to the Omani Navy in 1979.

She takes trainees from all Omani uniformed organisations, including the military and the police service, and during her visits to port she acts as an ambassador for Oman; she has visited almost every part of the world during her service, including taking part in the Australian bicentennial celebration in 1988.

The current vessel is expected to be retired in 2014 and replaced with a new ship, which is being built in Romania. The new ship will be considerably larger – it is expected to be over 87 m in length – therefore providing more sail training berths.

Tip: A number of her sails, including the square sails on her foremast, carry the national symbol of Oman, a red dagger and crossed swords.

'Bluff your way' fact: *Shabab Oman* has won the Friendship Trophy, perhaps the most coveted of the Tall Ship Races trophies, more often than any other ship.

Party spirit on *Shabab* with a band on the deckhouse and the crew dancing.

Shabab Oman leaving Aarhus without her distinctive sails set.

Shabab Oman with her distinctive sail markings.

Shtandart

Russian Ship (fully rigged ship)

Website: www.shtandart.com

Crew	Cadets/Trainees	POR	Type	LOA
6	19	St Petersburg	Replica	34.5m

Shtandart is a replica of Peter the Great's flagship *Shtandart* from 1703. Although the original plans were lost, research carried out in the 1980s for The Hermitage Museum and an eighteenth-century engraving of the original ship were combined to produce the design. She was built between 1994 and 1999 and her maiden voyage was in June 2000.

Her rich design is typical of ships of the era. Her stern carries images from Russian sea battles and the lion represents power. Although the original ship carried twenty-eight cannon, the replica has just five, which are used on ceremonial occasions.

She operates throughout Europe, and berths are available on board for Tall Ships Races in the summer and voyages in the Canary Islands in the winter.

Tip: Look for her high bowsprit and broad yellow panel. The figurehead and decorative stern are unmistakable.

'Bluff your way' fact: The Siberian larch that was used to build her was from a forest that was planted in 1703 and intended to be used to build a great navy for Peter the Great. The same wood was used in the building of the Jubilee Sailing Trust's ship *Tenacious*.

Above left: Shtandart figurehead.

Above right: Shtandart motoring.

Shtandart's stern, showing her name and port of registration in Russian.

Simon Bolivar

Venezuelan Barque

Website: www.armada.mil.ve

Crew	Cadets/Trainees	POR	Type	LOA
110	87	La Guaira	New build	86m

Built in Bilbao, Spain, and commissioned into the Venezuelan navy in 1980, she has three half sisters, the Mexican *Cuauhtémoc*, the Colombian *Gloria* and the Ecuadorian *Guayas*.

She is operated as a military vessel with the official registration BE11, and is a training ship for cadets from the Venezuelan Armada (Navy) Military Academy, as well as the navy's flagship. She regularly participates in the South American regattas and races, and on several occasions has crossed the Atlantic to join the European events. She is often distinguished by the huge Venezuelan 'battle flag' flown from her stern.

Her figurehead is a male figure draped in the national flag.

She is named after the South American political and military leader who led Venezuela, and other Latin American countries, to independence from Spain. There is no connection between this ship and an earlier vessel called *Simon Bolivar*, a Dutch passenger liner that sank off Harwich in 1939.

Tip: Like several other vessels, her paint scheme depicts mock gun ports but in the reverse colours with black 'ports' on a white hull. Her name appears only on the stern.

'Bluff your way' fact: She spent six years in refit between 2002 and 2008.

Simon Bolivar alongside in Halifax.

Simon Bolivar under sail.

Simon Bolivar figurehead.

Sørlandet

Norwegian Ship (fully rigged ship)

Website: www.sorlandet.org

Crew	Cadets/Trainees	POR	Type	LOA
15	70	Kristiansand	New build	64m

Sørlandet was built in 1927 as a sail-training ship for boys at the southern Norway maritime training school. Although her website and publicity material claim that she is the oldest original square-rigged sailing ship still operating, this record probably belongs to another Norwegian ship, *Statsraad Lehmkuhl*. However, *Sørlandet* has retained her original name, unlike many others.

Her programme usually includes the European Tall Ship Races, three-day fjord cruises and transatlantic voyages to spend the winter in the Caribbean. For periods in 2012, 2013 and 2014, she was on charter to the Canadian organisation Class Afloat, which takes high school students to sea for up to ten months on a programme combining academic studies with seamanship. Class Afloat previously used the Canadian vessel *Concordia*, which sank in 2010.

Tip: She has no figurehead, and her name is shown both along her bow and on her stern.

'Bluff your way' fact: When *Sørlandet* took part in the first Tall Ships Race in 1956, she was the only one of the square riggers not yet fitted with an engine, and was therefore towed out to the open sea.

Head to head in the record books. *Sørlandet* (on the right) and *Statsraad Lehmkuhl.*

Name on *Sørlandet*'s stern.

Sørlandet under sail.

Spirit of New Zealand

New Zealand Barquentine

Website: www.spiritofadventure.org.nz

Crew	Cadets/Trainees	POR	Type	LOA
14	40	Auckland	New build	45.2m

The *Spirit of New Zealand* was commissioned in 1986 as a second ship for the Spirit of Adventure Trust. The first ship, a Topsail Schooner, was retired in 1997, and *Spirit of New Zealand* now operates a busy schedule for 340 days of the year.

Her programme is based on the classic sail-training concept, using the unique environment of the ship for youth development. The focus of learning is on teamwork, developing skills of communication, self-reliance, self-discipline, self-esteem, resilience, confidence and leadership. Learning to sail a tall ship is only a small part of the experience for those on board.

The places for her main programme of ten-day voyages are allocated through schools, with individuals applying for one of their school's allocated berths. There is also a five-day programme, for which the crew is made up of groups from different schools competing to gain the most points for participation, problem-solving, teamwork and aquatic sports.

Her programme is largely based out of Auckland (her home port), Wellington and the Bay of Islands. In 2013 she was one of a number of international ships that visited Australia for the Royal Australian Navy centenary celebrations and International Fleet Review.

Tip: Her bow carries the New Zealand silver fern leaf in white on an all-black hull.

'Bluff your way' fact: Although the bunks were designed to take twenty males and twenty females, sleeping in separate accommodation, a change was made to so that six of the male bunks could be separated. This allows her to sail with twenty-six females and fourteen males, and was a response to the number of female applicants frequently being higher than that of male applicants.

The New Zealand silver fern.

Spirit of New Zealand in Sydney.

Spirit of New Zealand under sail.

Stad Amsterdam

Dutch Ship (fully rigged ship)

Website: www.stadamsterdam.com

Crew	Cadets/Trainees	POR	Type	LOA
25	56	Amsterdam	New build	76m

The ship was commissioned jointly for the City of Amsterdam and the employment agency Randstad, and the build offered work experience and educational opportunities for young people from the city who had dropped out of school. Her design is based on the classic clippers such as *Cutty Sark*.

The ship sails all over the world: during the summer months she can usually be found in the waters around Europe, often at the major festivals. Later in the year she makes the transatlantic crossing to the eastern seaboard of North America and the Caribbean, to return to Europe in the spring. Her summer voyages are closer to traditional sail training, with the opportunity to get involved in all aspects of sailing the ship. Her Caribbean season is billed as luxury cruising with a more relaxed atmosphere.

Stad Amsterdam's bell. (Photo Sander Stoepker)

Tip: Her black hull has one thin white line and two gold ones.

'Bluff your way' fact: Young people joining the voyages can train in seamanship and also for the hospitality trade during luxury cruises and day sails as part of a project with Randstad.

Above left: Stern view.

Above right: Stad Amsterdam figurehead.

Stad Amsterdam under sail.

Statsraad Lehmkuhl

Norwegian Barque

Website: www.lehmkuhl.no

Crew	Cadets/Trainees	POR	Type	LOA
17	150	Bergen	New build	98m

The *Statsraad Lehmkuhl* has had a complicated history. She was built in 1914 as a training ship for the German merchant marine; her original name was *Grossherzog Friedrich August*. During most of the First World War she was used as a stationary training ship in Germany, and after the war she was taken as a prize by the UK but not put to work.

In 1923 she was sold to the Norwegian Shipowners Association and renamed *Statsraad Lehmkuhl*, after the Cabinet Minister Kristofer Lehmkuhl who instigated the purchase. She operated sail-training programmes for the Bergen School Ship Foundation in Norway between 1924 and 1966, except for a few years during the Second World War, when she was captured by the Germans and renamed *Westwarts*.

She was bought again in 1967 by a private shipowner, and operated sail-training voyages, mainly for the shipowner's company, until the oil crisis in 1973 made her uneconomic and he donated her to her current owners, The Statsraad Lehmkuhl Tall Ship Foundation.

Although many voyages are open to the public, she undertakes a number of longer trips each year as training for cadets of the Norwegian Navy. She can be seen in many European festivals, races and regattas during the summer.

Tip: Although her hull is white, the blue paintwork below the waterline is usually visible.

'Bluff your way' fact: When in use by the Norwegian navy, she sails as KNM (equivalent to the British HMS) *Statsraad Lehmkuhl*.

Statsraad coming in to Lerwick.

Statsraad Lehmkuhl.

Statsraad under sail.

Tarangini

Indian Barque

Website: www.indiannavy.nic.in/naval-fleet/sail-training-ships

Crew	Cadets/Trainees	POR	Type	LOA
21	35	Kochi	New build	54m

Tarangini was designed by the British Naval Architect Colin Mudie and built in Goa, India; she was commissioned into the Indian navy as a sail-training ship in 1997. She is a sister ship to the British *Lord Nelson*, with the same hull and rig, although she has a different internal layout. The name *Tarangini* is Sanskrit, and means 'full of waves'.

   Although seldom seen in Europe, she took part in the 2005 European Tall Ship Races. In 2003 she joined the American Great Lakes series during her circumnavigation of the world.

Tip: Her name can be difficult to spot; it is written in black on the extended gold wings of the swan figurehead. Her most distinguishing feature is a shelf-like platform at the stern.

'Bluff your way' fact: Her badge depicts two swans, one teaching the other to fly over waves, representing the training role of the ship. This is mirrored in her figurehead, which is a stylised golden swan.

Above left: *Tarangini*'s badge.

Above right: *Tarangini* coming alongside in Halifax with her yards manned.

Tarangini in Parade of Sail followed by *Prince William* (now *Rah Naward*) and *Picton Castle*.

Tenacious

British three-masted Barque

Website:www.jst.org.uk

Crew	Cadets/Voyage Crew	POR	Type	LOA
8	40	Southampton	New build	66.56m

Built in Southampton, *Tenacious*'s first voyage was in 2000. At the time, she was the largest wooden-hulled ship to be built in the UK for over 100 years and was made from Siberian larch. She is operated by a UK charity called the Jubilee Sailing Trust, whose mission is the integration of both able-bodied and disabled people through tall ship sailing. *Tenacious* was built by the trust using a mixture of able-bodied and disabled volunteers. The trust provides adventurous team-building holidays to people over sixteen with no upper age limit. Her trainees, referred to as voyage crew, are made up of 50 per cent able-bodied people and 50 per cent people with a range of physical disabilities.

Tenacious can often be found at maritime festivals in Northern Europe and sometimes takes part in the Tall Ships Races. In the winter she usually operates in the warmer seas of the the Mediterranean, the Canary Islands or the Caribbean.

Tip: If you see a wheelchair user aloft you are almost certainly either looking at *Tenacious* or *Lord Nelson*. Look out for the 'lubbers hole' on *Tenacious*, an easy access to the platforms.

'Bluff your way' fact: *Tenacious* has a speaking compass to allow blind crew members to take the helm, and the wheel can be replaced with a joystick for those with limited strength or dexterity.

Above left: *Tenacious* is one of only two fully accessible Class A tall ships – the other is *Lord Nelson* (see p. 108). Both are operated by the UK-based sailing charity, The Jubilee Sailing Trust.

Above right: Wheelchair user aloft.

Tenacious with sails set.

Thalassa

Dutch Barquentine

Website: www.tallshipthalassa.nl

Crew	Cadets/Trainees	POR	Type	LOA
5	36	Harlingen	New build	47.25m

Thalassa was built in 1980 as a modern fishing vessel, and operated in the English Channel and the North Sea with the name *Relinquenda*.

In August 1984 she collided with a Second World War wreck; her damaged hull was salvaged and sold, but the new owner went bankrupt and the planned conversion to a yacht never happened.

In 1994 she was sold again, this time to Arnold Hylkema and Henk Stallinga, who repaired the hull and converted her to a traditionally rigged sailing ship. She was renamed after the sea goddess Thalassa of Greek mythology. She was relaunched in 1995 and, although she took part in her first Tall Ships Race in 2004, her main function is for charters and passenger trips. Arnold Hylkema still sails as captain.

Her bow and figurehead.

Tip: Her navy blue hull and curved line, with the white super structure at her stern, help identify her from a distance. Close up you can see her mermaid figurehead.

'Bluff your way' fact: As well as adventure sailing, *Thalassa* runs special 'whisky voyages' visiting the Scottish single malt distilleries with a well-stocked bar and resident whisky expert on board.

Thalassa under sail.

Thalassa heeling to port.

Thor Heyerdahl

German three-masted Topsail Schooner

Website: www.thor-heyerdahl.de

Crew	Cadets/Trainees	POR	Type	LOA
4	34	Kiel	Restoration	49.83m

Thor Heyerdahl was originally built as a freight carrier in 1930; although she was equipped with an engine from the beginning, she also carried sails for auxiliary power. During her first fifty years she also bore the names *Tinka, Marga Henning, Silke,* and *Minnow.*

In 1979 she was bought by two sailing enthusiasts, who turned the now rundown ship into a Topsail Schooner to use it for sail training, especially for teenagers and young adults. One of the two original owners had sailed with the Norwegian adventurer Thor Heyerdahl, most famous for his Kon Tiki expedition, and suggested that the ship should be named after him. Today the ship still operates a programme for young people aged fifteen to twenty-five, from all social classes and backgrounds. Winter voyages last up to six months and include academic and maritime instruction. In the summer she operates a typical sail-training programme open to a wider age group, and regularly appears at regattas and festivals.

Tip: With three masts and three square sails on her foremast she can easily be mistaken for a Barquentine.

'Bluff your way' fact: Thor Heyerdahl sailed for 101 days from Peru across the South Pacific in a small craft made of balsa wood in his famous Kon-tiki expedition.

Thor Heyerdahl sailing.

Ship Directory:
Vessels With Four or More Masts

The most common four-masted vessels are the four-masted Barques, but there are also fully rigged Ships and some without any square sails like the gaff-rigged Schooner *Santa Maria Manuela* from Portugal.

Other sailing ships with four or more masts include the sailing ships of the luxury Star Clipper line. More cruise ships than sailing ships, these are not included in the Ship Directory, as they are commercial passenger vessels sailed by the crew.

However, since this book is meant to help you identify tall ships, a couple of pictures are included here in case you see them.

Royal Clipper – a unique five-masted fully rigged ship.

Star Flyer and *Star Clipper* are both four-masted barquentines.

Creoula

Portuguese Schooner

Crew	Cadets/Trainees	POR	Type	LOA
46	52	Lisbon	Restoration	67.36m

The *Creoula* was built for the Portuguese Fisheries organisation in just sixty-two working days and was launched on 10 May 1937. She was employed as part of the 'white fleet' supporting cod fishing in Newfoundland and Greenland. The fishermen caught the cod from tiny boats called dories. In 1973, when she was no longer viable for fishing, she was acquired by the Portuguese government, and in 1987 began a new career as the second sail-training ship for the Portuguese navy, joining the Barque *Sagres*.

Although operated by the navy, the trainees on board *Creoula* are civilian youngsters and are selected from schools and other institutions, giving them the opportunity to find out about life at sea and maritime careers.

   Creoula rarely ventures far from Portugal.

Tip: Almost identical to her sister ship, *Santa Maria de Manuela*, the only obvious difference is the colour of the masts: *Creoula* has no white on hers.

'Bluff your way' fact: *Creoula* apeared on a Portuguese €0,80 stamp.

Above left: Depicted on a stamp.

Above right: Alongside.

Creoula on the Tagus in 2006.

 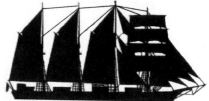

Esmeralda

Chilean four-masted Barquentine

Website: www.esmeralda.cl

Crew	Cadets/Trainees	POR	Type	LOA
300	90	Valparaiso	New build	113m

Esmeralda was originally designed to be Spain's national training ship but during her construction in 1947 the yard where she was being built suffered catastrophic explosions, which severely damaged the ship, and work was stopped. In 1950, Spain and Chile were in negotiation about the debt owed to Chile as a result of the Spanish Civil War. The debt was repaid with manufactured products, which included the partly finished *Esmeralda*. She was finally launched in 1953.

Her sister ship is the training ship for the Spanish navy, the four-masted Topsail Schooner *Juan Sebastián Elcano*. Originally they had the same sail plan until, in the 1970s, *Esmeralda*'s rigging was changed to her current arrangement as a four-masted Barquentine.

Although she has taken part in the Tall Ships Races, she is not a regular visitor to Europe and can usually be found in South American and Caribbean waters. Her nickname is La Dama Blanca ('The White Lady).

Tip: Her hull is green below the waterline and this same paint scheme appears on her boats and deck fittings.

'Bluff your way' fact: There were reports that claimed the ship was used as a kind of a floating jail and torture chamber for political prisoners of the Augusto Pinochet regime from 1973 to 1980. It is claimed that over a hundred people were kept there at times, and this has sometimes caused her arrival in port to be controversial.

Esmeralda's foredeck.

Under sail (note the green of the hull).

Kruzenshtern

Russia four-masted Barque

Website: www.bgarf.ru/en/kruzenshtern

Crew	Cadets/Trainees	POR	Type	LOA
70	164	Kailiningrad	Restoration	113.49m

Kruzenshtern was built in 1926, originally called *Padua*, and was one of the famous German P-liners. She was awarded to Russia in 1946 as part of the war reparations following the Second World War and renamed *Kruzenshtern* after the famous Russian hydrographer and navigator. Today she is operated by the State Baltic Academy of the Fisheries as a training ship, although she takes paying passengers to help fund her operating costs.

Kruzenshtern operates mainly in Northern Europe, spending parts of every year in her home waters of the Baltic. However, she can also be found in the festival ports and as part of the Tall Ships Races during the summer. She sometimes travels further afield to the Canary Islands, the Mediterranean and Canada.

Tip: The hull is black, white and red, representing the colours of the old German Empire flag, a reminder that she was once part of the Flying P-line. In the same way as several other modern tall ships, she also has mock gun ports incorporated into her paint scheme.

'Bluff your way' fact: Other ships of the Flying P-line included *Pamir*, which sank in 1957; *Passat*, which is now tied up and used as a youth camp in Travemunde, Germany; *Pommern*, which is in Mariehann, Finland; and *Peking*, which is a museum ship in New York City.

Kruzenshtern is the second-largest Class A vessel currently sailing. The biggest is *Sedov*.

Above left: Painting of *Padua* under sail.

Above right: Her name is written in Cyrillic script on her bow; this is how it appears.

Santa Maria Manuela

Portuguese Schooner

Website: www.santamariamanuela.pt

Crew	Cadets/Trainees	POR	Type	LOA
22	50	Aveiro	Restoration	68.64m

Santa Maria Manuela was originally launched in 1937 and was part of the Portuguese cod fishing fleet. In 1993 she was more or less abandoned and left to rot despite a large-scale attempt to raise funds to return her to sea. In 2007 the hull was bought by a Portuguese company, Pascoal & Filhos, who completely restored her to her original design as a four-masted gaff-rigged Schooner. She retains the traditional white hull from the Portuguese White Fleet, which operated off Newfoundland and Greenland until the early 1990s.

Today, sailing on board is open to anyone. The minimum age for sailing is fourteen (or fifteen for races), although young people under eighteen need to be accompanied by an adult. She sails mainly in southern European waters, but she does take part in Tall Ships Races and festivals, especially those in the Mediterranean.

Tip: *Santa Maria Manuela* is almost identical to her sister ship *Creoula*, which is operated as a training ship for the Portuguese navy. Check the name along the bow or on the stern! The only obvious difference from a distance is the white section, where the upper and lower sections of the mast join on *Santa Maria Manuela*. On *Creoula* this is the same colour as the mast.

'Bluff your way' fact: The steel used for her hull had been originally destined for a Portuguese military vessel; it was used to build *Santa Maria Manuela* and a sister ship *Creoula*. The high-quality materiel probably helped her hull survive the years of neglect.

Above: Alongside in Bremerhaven.

Right: Under sail in Lisbon.

Sedov

Russian four-masted Barque

Website: www.sts-sedov.info

Crew	Cadets/Trainees	POR	Type	LOA
156	46	Murmansk	Restoration	117.5m

Sedov was launched in 1921 as the German vessel *Magdalene Vinnen* (named for a member of the shipbuilder's family) and was one of the earliest sailing ships to carry an auxiliary engine. Although primarily a cargo vessel, she also carried cadets from her early days. She was later sold and renamed the *Kommodore Johnsen* but retained her joint cargo and officer cadet training role.

As with other German ships, she formed part of Second World War reparations and was given to the Soviet Union. She is operated by Murmansk State Technical University.

Tip: Sedov carries six sails on each square rigged mast.

'Bluff your way' fact: *Sedov* has been frequently targeted by unpaid creditors of the Russian Federation. On several occasions she has had to leave port quickly to avoid being served with a writ and has also missed some festivals for the same reason.

Sedov's name in Cyrillic script.

Sedov with full sail.

GONE BUT NOT FORGOTTEN

There have been some tall ships that have remained in people's memories long after they have gone. Some are part of history, like the clippers *Cutty Sark* and *Thermopylae*. Some are remembered for other reasons, such as the *Pamir*, which went down in 1957 with the loss of eighty men. Sometimes, like the British three-masted Schooners, the *Winston Churchill* and *Malcolm Miller*, operated by the Sail Training Association (now the Tall Ships Youth Trust),

Concordia, with her maple leaf adorned sails.

it is because so many people have had positive experiences when they sailed on them or saw them taking part in races and festivals.

Even today some ships are well known only because they have come to the end of their life in a dramatic way. In 1984 the *Marques* sank while sailing from Bermuda during a Tall Ships Race with a significant loss of life. More recent examples include the Canadian vessel *Concordia*, which sank 300 miles off Brazil in 2010. At the time, the ship was running a Class Afloat schools programme. The eight crew, eight teachers, and forty-eight trainees spent over forty hours in life rafts before all being rescued safely.

A couple of years earlier, in 2008, the Irish sail-training ship *Asgard II* sank in the Bay of Biscay, probably after hitting a submerged object. Despite a popular campaign, she has not been raised, although divers found her and carried out an investigation. Again all the crew and young people were rescued.

In 2013, three well-publicised incidents saw the loss of three ships. The HMS *Bounty* replica sank when caught in the path of Hurricane Sandy, with the loss of two lives. Also the pretty Brig *Astrid* sank in July 2013 after being forced onto rocks off the coast of Ireland; fortunately everyone on board was able to reach safety. She was raised successfully but it is unlikely that she will be restored to sail again. The third tragedy was the sinking of the *Wyvern* (a Class B vessel) during the 2013 Tall Ships Race; although the crew managed to escape, one life was

Asgard at sea.

Astrid after being raised from the water.

tragically lost when a crew member from the Class A Topsail Schooner *Wylde Swan* went down with the ship while trying to help.

All over the world you can find tall ships that have been restored as floating museums, too many to mention here. Some of them go to sea and many of them allow the public on board. Originally these museum ships were seen as a way of preserving what was thought to be a piece of maritime history. However, these days the tall ships are enjoying a renaissance, with new vessels being built and going to sea every year.

Not only are the tall ships not forgotten, they are not gone!

All you need to do now is go out and find them.

WANT TO GET INVOLVED?

If you want to get involved with tall ships, there are many opportunities. Of course, sailing on a ship is the best way, but you can also help with maintenance, become a volunteer, support fundraising or join the many 'friends' organisations.

The best starting point is usually to find a ship that interests you and that operates in your home area. In this book you will find details of many of the ships' websites, where they will have information about available berths and sailing programmes. They can usually be contacted either to book a berth or to volunteer to help out in other ways. Many of the ships also have day sails during the summer season, and this is a good way to find out if a life at sea is for you!

Alternatively, most countries have a national sail-training organisation, and the ships from that country will almost all be members. If you start with the international umbrella body www.sailtraininginternational.org, you will find links from there to the national organisations, who will put you in touch with individual operators.

There are also several agencies who fill berths for a number of ships, and they will generally have a list of ships with berths available for Tall Ships Races.

Finally, if the ships are coming to a port near you, the festival organisers will be looking for volunteers to help host the ships and the visiting crew.

Mir (foreground) and the Tall Ships in Bremerhaven.

A relaxed day sail on *Gulden Leeuw*.

Above: Museum ship HMS *Najaden*, Halmstad, Sweden.

Right: Helping with maintenance on *Tenacious*.

Working aloft. (*JST*)

INDEX

SHIP RIGGING IDENTIFICATION

1. Bowsprit
2. Martingale
3. Figurehead
4. Flying Jib
5. Outer jib
6. Inner jib
7. Fore topmast staysail
8. Foremast
9. Fore royal
10. Fore upper topgallant sail
11. Fore lower topgallant sail

12. Fore upper topsail
13. Fore lower topsail
14. Foresail, Fore course
15. Main royal staysail
16. Main topgallant staysail
17. Main middle staysail
18. Main topmast staysail
19. Mainmast
20. Main royal
21. Main upper topgallant sail

22. Main lower topgallant sail
23. Main upper topsail
24. Main lower topsail
25. Mainsail, Main course
26. Mizzen royal staysail
27. Mizzen topgallant staysail
28. Mizzen middle staysail
29. Mizzen topmast staysail
30. Mizzen mast
31. Mizzen royal

32. Mizzen upper topgallant sail
33. Mizzen lower topgallant sail
34. Mizzen upper topsail
35. Mizzen lower topsail
36. Crossjack, Mizzen course
37. Jigger topgallant staysail
38. Jigger topmast staysail
39. Jigger staysail
40. Jigger mast
41. Gaff topsail
42. Spanker

Image courtesy of American Sail Training Association, www.sailtraining.org.